Of

Terms

Elizabeth King

veddy British

1997

Chambers Commercial Reference

© W & R Chambers Ltd Edinburgh, 1987

Published by W & R Chambers Ltd Edinburgh, 1987

British Library Cataloguing in Publication Data
King, Elizabeth
    Office technology terms.—(Chambers commercial reference)
   1. Office practice—Automation—Dictionaries
   I. Title
   651   HF5548.2
ISBN 0 550 18063 X

Typeset by Blackwood Pillans & Wilson Ltd.
Printed in Singapore by Singapore National Printers Ltd.

Preface

Office Technology Terms is a compact but comprehensive reference book which has been specially written to meet the needs of school and college students on a wide range of business and vocational courses at intermediate level.

Along with the other titles in the Chambers Commercial Reference series, *Office Technology Terms* provides up-to-date explanations of the key terms used in various areas of business activity. All words and abbreviations are listed alphabetically and defined in clear simple English.

Although intended as a companion to course studies, *Office Technology Terms* is also an ideal reference text for those already working in a commercial environment. The book will prove to be an invaluable companion to their work.

Other titles in this series

Business Terms
Bookkeeping and Accounting Terms
Office Practice Terms

Office Technology Terms
Elizabeth King lectures in information processing and computer
literacy at Oldham College of Technology.

Aa

AA Handbook   A handbook produced by the Automobile Association which gives details of the services of the organisation as well as information about hotels, garages, half-day closing for shops and some maps. It can be useful when planning business trips and itineraries and when booking accommodation. A similar publication is produced by the RAC.

abbreviated dialling   Telephone numbers which are called on a regular basis can be obtained by dialling two or three digits instead of the full number of digits in the dialling code and subscriber's number. A computer controlled exchange may be programmed to dial numbers automatically when only two or three digits are dialled. This facility is particularly useful when overseas numbers are dialled frequently.

abort   In computing, to abandon an activity usually because an error has been made, or because there has been program or system failure.

absent extension answering   When an incoming telephone call to an extension is not answered within several rings, the call can be automatically transferred or re-routed to another, pre-arranged extension. If this second extension does not answer, then the process may be repeated several times.

access   The term used to indicate gaining control of a computer system or the retrieval of data from a storage device (e.g. main memory) or peripheral unit (e.g. magnetic disk drive). Access can be used either as a verb or a noun.

access time   The time taken to retrieve data or information from a storage device. Access times can vary according to the type of storage device used, e.g. access time from a magnetic disk is shorter than from magnetic tape. See also **random access** and **serial access**.

accumulator The memory location in the computer in which data is temporarily stored whilst it is being processed, e.g. a number can be temporarily called from the accumulator and another number added to it, subtracted from it or compared with it.

acoustic coupler A device which converts electrical pulses from a key operated machine to sound (acoustic waves) for transmission and reception along telephone lines to and from a computer, permitting computers to be connected along these lines with a terminal by a modem and telephone handset.

acoustic hood A cover usually made of plastic placed over the ribbon casing and printing point of a printer which reduces the noise level. Acoustic hoods are particularly important in environments where the printer is constantly operative.

ADC Advice of duration and charge. A service offered by the telephone operator which enables the duration of a telephone call to be metered and costed. A fee is payable for this service in addition to the charge for the call.

address As information is entered into a computer, each place in which the information is stored has an address. That address alters as information is moved around. An address is itself a number.

addressing machine An office machine which duplicates information from masters, printing one or a few copies of each of a series of masters. It is used when standard information needs to be duplicated at regular intervals. The original purpose for the machine was the duplicating of a series of names and addresses but it can be put to other uses. There are three main types; embossed metal plate which prints through an inked ribbon; stencil frame, cut by a special fitment on the platen of a typewriter and spirit process machine, the master copies of which are made with hectographic carbon paper.

adding machine There are two main kinds of adding machine; the listing/adding machine which gives a printed record of all calculations on a tally roll and the non-listing adding machine which records the totals in dials on the machine only.

advice of duration and charge See **ADC**.

agenda A programme for a forthcoming business meeting, which sets out the title of the meeting, the venue, date and time and lists the items to be discussed in numbered order. An agenda is circulated before the meeting to all persons invited to attend.

airmail Mail carried by air. The cost of airmail tends to be rather high, so a lightweight paper is used for correspondence, approximately $25-30$ gm^2.

airway letters Letters carried by air to regular destinations, accepted by British Airways at certain airport offices; first class letters will be taken on the next available direct flight to the destination airport.

alarm call A service offered by British Telecom whereby a subscriber can ask to be called at a specific time during the day or night, e.g. early in the morning for an important business appointment.

ALGOL Algorithmic orientated language. A high level computer programming language used especially for scientific and mathematical applications.

algorithmic orientated language See **ALGOL**.

alphabetical filing The simplest classification for filing where documents are filed according to the first letters in the name and then in order of the second names, e.g. an organisation's own telephone directory will list the names of clients and suppliers in alphabetical order.

alphanumeric An acronym formed from the words alphabetic and numeric. Alphanumeric refers to those keys on a keyboard that represent letters and numbers rather than symbols and special functions. An alphanumeric keyboard is one similar to that on a typewriter or computer.

ALU Arithmetic and logic unit. The microprocessor in the central processing unit of the computer which carries out the arithmetic and logical operations required by an input command e.g. comparison of two numbers.

American standard code for information interchange An international standard computer code in which eight binary bits are combined to represent letters, numbers and symbols on a computer keyboard. Most VDUs and printers use this code. See also **ASCII**.

analogue A continuously varying quantity e.g. temperature, time. When analogue quantities are measured and given a numerical value, they become digital. Compare **digital**.

answer back code In the installation of a telex, each machine is equipped with an answer back code, which is an individual set of characters by which it can identify itself and be identified. Each telex subscriber can choose a code name which is then printed in the Post Office telex directory.

answer-recording machine A telephone answer-recording machine may be switched on instead of the telephone at the close of business. The caller will hear a pre-recorded message which may be changed if required. After hearing the pre-recorded message, a caller can be asked to leave his/her name and telephone number (and any message that he/she may want to leave). The recorded message can then be played back when the office opens.

answering machine A telephone answering machine may be switched on instead of the telephone after the close of business. Any caller will hear a pre-recorded message which may be changed if required.

anti-static Not attracting positively charged electric ions e.g. dust. Disk wallets are usually anti-static and therefore protect the disk from contamination by dust.

aperture card A card (punched or edge-punched) made up of 80 columns which has a frame of microfilm inserted and which can be used to form an index, sorted via the punched holes. Once sorted, more information is available on the inserted microfilm.

applications software A computer program or set of programs designed to carry out specific tasks e.g. a business application, a game, word processing, data analysis. Applications software is distinct from systems software which controls the operation of the total computer. Compare **systems software**.

archive (1) To archive is the process of storing data files on a computer in a retrievable form e.g. hard or floppy disk. (2) Archives are files stored on hard or floppy disk, usually data files.

arithmetic and logic unit See **ALU**.

ASCII See **American standard code for information interchange**.

ASR Automatic send and receive, sometimes referred to as answer, send and receive. A teletypewriter and receiver used in conjunction with a computer.

assemble To convert a machine language program from a symbolic language program.

assembler A computer program which converts a symbolic language program automatically into a machine language program which can then be directly executed by the computer.

assembly language A programming language in which each statement corresponds to a machine language instruction. An assembly language is usually given some form of mnemonic e.g. BASIC, COBOL.

asynchronous transmission In the transmission of data, asynchronous transmission occurs when time intervals between characters transmitted are of unequal length. This form of communication with other devices does not require a continuous exchange of synchronisation signals. Compare **synchronous transmission**.

ATLAS (1) Automatic tabulating, listing and sorting system. A software package extensively used for tabulating, listing and sorting. (2) Automated telephone line address system. A storage bank, which the operator can use to store programmed numbers for required calls later in the day.

attention line The line in a letter which reads 'For the attention of. . . .' which is used to bring the contents of the letter to the attention of a particular employee of the organisation, although addressed to the organisation as a whole.

audio conferencing A facility which allows several sub-scribers to be connected to one telephone call so that they all may take part in the same conversation or conference. Also referred to as **conference call**.

audio typing Documents (e.g. letters, memoranda, reports) are dictated onto a dictating machine (an electronic machine which records on one of various recording media, although usually, magnetic tape) so that a typist can then play back the recording and transcribe it on the typewriter.

automatic centring A facility of most word processors to automatically centre a line of text equally between the left and right margins when so required by the operator.

automatic dialling device There are several main types of automatic dialling device e.g. X-Press Callmaker, Tape Callmaker, Card Callmaker, although all operate on the basis of storage of numbers of the operator's choice for assisted dialling, saving time and reducing the possibility of error. Most offer a 'repeat last number' facility which is of benefit if the number is engaged or did not respond.

automatic document feeder A device attached to a printer which automatically feeds in a new single sheet of stationery when the old sheet has been printed.

automatic last-number re-dial A feature on some telephones where the last number dialled, if engaged or not responded to, can automatically be re-dialled by the depression of one special digit.

automatic pagination A feature of some word processors whereby the pages in a document are automatically numbered. Usually referred to as **pagination**.

automatic send and receive See **ASR**.

automatic tabulating, listing and sorting system See **ATLAS**.

automated telephone line address system A storage bank which the telephone operator can use to store programmed numbers for calls that are required later in the day. The operator will feed the STD or IDD codes and telephone numbers into the storage bank ready for use. Later in the day when calls are required, the operator can automatically dial the required call by pressing a button on the console.

automatic transfer A facility of some telephone extensions where a user who wishes to transfer a call to another extension can dial a code and the extension number required. The call is then automatically transferred without going through the main switchboard.

Bb

back-up copy   A copy made of the working disk sometimes done daily or weekly in the event of accident to the working disk so that all data is not lost completely. The back-up copy disks are normally stored in a separate area to the working disks.

background   Tasks which may be carried out by a computer while data is being input for a foreground task, e.g. a computer may be printing in background while editing is being carried out in the foreground.

backing storage   Storage media, such as magnetic disks apart from the computer's main memory. Data and programs held in backing storage have to be transferred into the core store before use. When the power is off, information in the backing storage is therefore not lost. The capacity of a backing storage memory is greater than the computer's internal working memory.

banda   Another name for spirit duplicator for which a master must be prepared by writing or typing on master paper with a sheet of hecto carbon placed against the glossy side of the paper. A reversed image is obtained on the back of the master paper and the prepared master is fixed to the drum of the banda (or duplicator) so that as sheets of duplicating paper are fed through, they are damped by a fluid which activates the dye on the master. The image is then transferred the correct way round onto the duplicating paper.

bank balance   The amount of money standing to the credit of a bank account. A bank balance computer program enables cash flow problems to be handled using stored information relating to income and expenditure. An organisation can use such a program to be advised of current transactions and warned of possible over-drawing.

bar code A code in the form of printed lines used on labels which identify and contain information about a product. Bar codes can be read by a wand, light pen or bar code scanner. An application is in the labelling of retail products where the wand is used to record the sale at the time and place of purchase. Bar codes are also sometimes used in libraries.

bar code reader Sometimes referred to as a bar code scanner, an optical device which can read data from documents and objects, bearing information recorded in the form of a pattern of printed lines. The characters are translated into digital signals for processing.

barred extensions Telephone extensions which may be barred from certain areas of use e.g. barred from Subscriber Trunk Dialling and/or International Direct Dialling. This facility is sometimes known as 'route restriction' or 'level 9 access barred'.

base A numerical value given to the structure of a counting system e.g. binary works in base two, decimal works in base ten.

BASIC Beginner's all-purpose symbolic instruction code. A high level programming language designed for use in a number of various forms for microcomputers. It is particularly suitable for entering and running programs on-line and is the most popular high level language for microcomputers.

batch A collection of computer transactions which are processed as a single unit.

batch processing The method of processing data by computer which groups together a collection of transactions and processes them as a single unit (a batch) rather than as individual items.

baud A unit of speed in telecommunications. The speed in bauds is the number of signal events per second.

baud rate A measure of the number of bits per second travelling from one part of a computer system e.g. a magnetic disk, to another part of the computer system, or between computers.

beginner's all-purpose symbolic instruction code See **BASIC**.

bi-directional printing The printing of lines both right to left and left to right, eliminating the need for a return to the beginning of the line. This speeds up the printing process.

binary A method of counting using only two alternative values; 1 or 0, on or off. Computer systems operate in binary.

bit A contraction for binary digit. The smallest unit of information used in a computer, having one of two values, 1 or 0. The central processing unit of a computer is often described according to the number of bits that it can process or access at one time e.g. 8 bit, 16 bit or 32 bit CPUs. Computers usually store information as a series of bits.

bits per second The number of bits of information that can be passed through telecommunication equipment in one second. The higher the number, the more expensive the equipment and the faster the speed of transmission over long distance connections. The lower the number, the cheaper the equipment, although charges for the telecommunication lines will rise because it will take more time to transmit or receive the same amount of information. Also known as **bps**.

black box The term given to a device which carries out a special function but whose detailed operation is unknown to the user.

block In computing, a group of records or information units handled as a single unit and stored in adjacent locations on magnetic tape or disk. In many magnetic storage devices only complete blocks can be accessed or transferred. The size of the block is determined by hardware considerations.

blocked style   The display style of a letter and the style most commonly used today in business letters. Each line starts at the left hand margin except sometimes for the date which is positioned to the left of the right margin for easy identification when filed. Headings do not need to be centred, paragraphs do not need to be indented and underscoring is considered unnecessary. The style is intended to save time as variations such as centring and underscoring take longer to type.

body   The part of a letter which transmits the message i.e. the text of a letter excluding the name, address, reference, salutation, etc.

bold face   A typeface which appears blacker than normal and is used for emphasis e.g. headings. When a bold face command is given to a printer, it is usual for the printing head to overtype the characters three or four times.

bond   A quality of paper generally used for letterheads and usually 80 gm^2.

boot   Short for **bootstrap**.

booting   Short for bootstrapping. This term is usually used to refer to the transfer of a disk operating system program from its storage on a disk to a computer's working memory.

bootstrap   A method of inputting data prior to the loading of a computer program in order that the program can be loaded.

box file   A folder used to house files. It is durable, capable of taking bulky items and storing many documents allowing easy access to and removal of the documents.

bpi   Bits per inch. A measurement for the density of data on a storage medium.

bps   Bits per second. The number of bits of information that can be passed through telecommunication equipment in one second.

bubble sort A method of ordering items in a list. Items are compared to a given criterion e.g. alphabetical order, then put into order. The process is repeated until the criterion is satisfied.

buffer (1) Memory space in a printer which stores the characters for printing. A printer with a buffer memory is capable of performing more complex printing functions than one that will only print characters as they are fed from the computer. (2) An area where data can be temporarily stored whilst being transferred from one unit to another e.g. data being written onto magnetic tape.

bug An error or defect in a computer system or computer program.

bulk storage The large volume storage of data and information on a storage device to which access times are relatively slow.

bundle A number of optical fibres grouped together within a single protective sheathing.

Business News Summary A telephone service which when dialled gives the day's trading on the stock market and which is updated at regular intervals during the day.

Business Reply Service A specially marked envelope supplied by the Post Office for which the sender of the letter pays no stamp fee. It is usually printed with the words 'No Stamp Required Licensee Will Pay Postage'. The fee is paid in turn by the addressee.

byte Perhaps short for *by eight*. The most common unit of computer storage, a byte is equivalent to one character, symbol or two numerical digits. A byte is a group of eight bits. One byte contains enough information to represent one ASCII character.

Cc

CAD   Computer aided design. The use of computers to aid design involving computer graphics, modelling, simulation, analysis of designs for production.

CAD/CAM   Computer aided design and manufacture. The use of computers to aid design and manufacturing processes. It can also include robotics and automated testing procedures.

CAE   Computer aided education. A term which covers CAI (computer aided instruction) and CAL (computer aided learning). The use of computers as teaching machines.

CAI   Computer aided instruction or computer assisted instruction. Refers to the use of computers as teaching machines.

CAL   Computer aided learning or computer assisted learning. Refers to the use of computers as teaching machines.

calculator   An electronic device capable of performing arithmetic functions and capable of displaying the results in windows. It has a simplified keyboard and complicated mathematical procedures can be activated by pressing a button built into the circuitry.

callback   A facility of modern telephone equipment where an extension user calling another extension which is engaged can press a button, replace the receiver and immediately the extension becomes free both telephone extensions will ring automatically. Also known as **camp on busy**.

call barring   Telephone extensions may be barred from certain areas of use e.g. barred from Subscriber Trunk Dialling and/or International Direct Dialling. Also known as **barred extensions**.

call diversion   A facility of modern telephone equipment whereby an extension can be 'programmed' so that when rung, the call is automatically diverted to another selected extension. This is of particular use when executives in meetings do not want to be interrupted; calls can be diverted to a given location for messages to be taken.

call metering   A device connected to a telephone console which records the number of units used by each extension of a PABX system. Usually found in hotels where guests may dial their own calls and have them charged to their account.

call waiting signal   A signal, either audible or visible, to a telephone extension user during an existing call which is used to inform him/her that another call to that extension is waiting.

Callmaker   A device for use in conjunction with a telephone, Callmaker operates on the principle of inputting telephone numbers into a store for simplified one or two digit dialling. Some offer inbuilt monitor loudspeakers and most Callmakers offer a 'repeat last number' facility. There are currently six types of Callmaker in circulation. See also **X-Press Callmaker, TD Callmaker, XL Callmaker, Card Callmaker, Tape Callmaker, Mono Callmaker**.

CAM   Computer aided manufacture. The use of computers to aid manufacturing processes. It can also include robotics and automated testing procedures.

camp on busy   The full title for this phrase is 'camp on busy/ring when free'. Upon finding an extension engaged, the user can dial a code that will queue his/her call and allows him/her to replace the receiver. When the engaged extension becomes free, both the caller's and the receiver's extensions will ring. Also known as **callback**.

cancel   A facility on some computers and word processors whereby the last command entered, or the last editing done, can be cancelled by the depression of the cancel (CAN) key.

caps lock   A facility of most electronic keyboards which locks the case of the letters typed into upper case. The *caps lock* key generally operates as a toggle switch i.e. struck once to lock letters into upper case and struck again to lock letters into lower case.

carbon   The term usually refers to carbon paper, one side of which is inked. A sheet of carbon is placed between the top copy and the flimsy copy of a letter before typing and an exact copy of the letter is produced on the flimsy paper. This copy is used for filing and is an inexpensive way of keeping records of outgoing correspondence and internal memoranda.

carbonless paper   Paper which has been chemically impregnated so that when the top sheet is struck an image is produced on second and subsequent sheets without the use of interleaved carbon paper. See also **NCR** paper.

card (punched card)   A card of a standard size, thickness and shape which is used to input data and instructions to an electronic device.

Card Callmaker   One of the types of Callmaker facility offered by British Telecom and used to save time and reduce the possibility of error in the telephone dialling process. In advance the operator punches out a permanent card for each number he or she wishes to store. Calls are made by lifting the handset, selecting the card required and slotting it into the Callmaker. Cards are made by using a special template and punch which are supplied with the Callmaker.

card index   A method of filing intended to make it easier to refer to any particular record in a filing system e.g. purchase invoices may be filed under an internal reference number, but an alphabetical index by clients' names may also be maintained which will quote the purchase invoice numbers when not known. Also known as **visible card index**.

card phone   A facility offered by British Telecom whereby a user purchases a card similar to the standard credit card for a variable sum offering various numbers of units. When a card is inserted into a special public telephone called a *card* *phone* and the caller is connected to the required number, available units are automatically deducted from the card. Cards can be renewed at most main Post Offices.

card punch A device which punches holes or perforates cards in specified locations upon instruction from a computer or a user at a keyboard in such a way that the information on the cards can be read by a card reader and converted back into information.

card reader A device which reads the perforations punched on cards (by means of brushes) and then converts this information into electronic messages.

carriage return A key on an electronic typewriter or computer keyboard which when depressed ends a line of type and returns the cursor or the printing point to the start of the next line.

carrier sensing An activity which operates around broadcast network. The transmission system has to ensure that terminals do not begin to transmit a message while a previous transmission is in progress and has also to ensure that simultaneous starts of transmission do not occur. The provision of this collision detection procedure, ensuring that transmissions are properly staggered, is called carrier sensing.

cartridge A chip containing software so designed that it can be plugged directly into a microcomputer so that the program contained in the chip becomes available on the computer. In computing jargon, referred to as a **dongle**.

cash on delivery See **COD**.

cassette A small sealed portable container used to hold magnetic tape or film (video cassette).

cassette tape An inexpensive way of storing programs or data for use on a microcomputer, although programs are very slow to record and play back.

16

cathode ray tube/cathode ray terminal A screen similar to a television screen which displays text from a computer. As keys are struck by the operator, letters or symbols appear on the screen. Screens normally have a black or dark green background, displaying white, pale green or amber characters. In graphics a variety of colours can be available.

Ceefax® A form of viewdata and the BBC's broadcast screen information service. Data to be displayed on the screen of a suitable television set is sent via a television signal.

central processing unit (CPU) The part of the computer system which co-ordinates the whole system, where all parts of the computer system are linked together and where the calculations and manipulation of data take place. It contains the ALU, the core memory and the control unit which directs and co-ordinates the operation of the computer and peripheral units. It interprets and executes computer programs, carrying out the processing of data.

centralised system The bringing together of an activity into one location. This can for example mean filing systems, computer based information systems, dictation systems. It has been suggested that when an activity is centralised the most efficient use of equipment takes place and progress and speed of work is increased.

centring A facility of most word processors which enables the operator to type a line of text which can if required be centred automatically between the left and right hand margins without the necessity of counting spaces and word lengths.

character A generic expression for a letter of the alphabet, a number, a symbol or a punctuation mark which a computer can print or display on a screen.

characters per inch See **cpi**.

characters per second See **cps**.

17

character reader A device which automatically inputs printed characters into a computer. Also known as **optical character recognition** and **magnetic ink character recognition**.

character recognition The use of recognition techniques so that a character reader can identify characters, usually alphanumeric. There are several types of technique, e.g. **magnetic ink character recognition, optical character recognition.**

character set The collection of numbers, letters, symbols and graphics that can be generated by a particular computer system.

cheap rate calls Telephone calls made after 6 pm and before 8 am Monday to Friday and at weekends at a reduced rate. Compare **standard rate calls** and **peak rate calls**.

chip A single integrated circuit formed on the surface of a piece of silicon etched with tiny electronic circuits. It is between 1 and 5 centimetres in length and can have between 6 and 40 external connections. A chip is used in computer systems and is sometimes referred to as a logic chip.

chronological order A method of filing whereby documents are filed in order of date. This system is rarely used on its own but it can be a usual method of filing papers inside individual filing folders.

circuit In telecommunications, a means of two-way communication which provides for transmission in each direction.

circuit switching In telecommunications, individual circuits are inter-connected to establish a continuous end-to-end connection (via successive exchanges) so that transmission is possible in each direction. Also called line switching. Contrast with **packet switching**.

circular A letter. There are two types of circular letter: (1) giving information. (2) seeking custom. In either case, the opening sentence must catch the reader's attention to sustain his/her interest. This opening sentence is often referred to as the 'punch line'.

City Link A collection and delivery service of packets and parcels offered by British Rail which uses both road and rail. Parcels collected at short notice can be sent by scheduled parcel trains which run at high speed and are delivered against a signature as proof of delivery. Special rates are available for regular dispatching.

classified directory A privately published telephone directory which lists local businesses, trades and organisations in alphabetical order of the trade or profession.

co-axial cable A cable used in communications which consists of an inner central conductor usually of copper, insulated from an outer conductor, also usually of copper. When high frequencies are passed down such a cable there is very low loss of energy. Several cables can be combined into a single bundle.

COBOL Common business orientated language. A high level computer programming language designed for use in business applications and the manipulation of business data, using terms which are related to ordinary English words.

COD Cash on delivery. A term used to refer to when goods are ordered and delivered, and are paid for by the recipient at the time of delivery.

code A machine language representation of a character e.g. ASCII.

cold start A complete restart of a computer following major failure or breakdown.

collating machine A labour-saving device used in the production of multiple copies of documents. As documents are copied, a collating machine bundles each document set together in chronological order of copying. In more expensive machines, an attachment for stapling, crimping or binding completed sets is incorporated into the collator.

COM Computer output microfilm. Sometimes called computer output microfiche. Instead of producing paper output, COM systems reduce the same information to microfilm (or microfiche). COM output systems are more economical than paper, as microfilm cost is 20% less than that of equivalent paper costs. Storage and distribution problems are also reduced because of the increased storage capacity of microfilm or microfiche.

command Any direct instruction to a computer which it will carry out immediately.

command key A special key or set of keys on a computer keyboard which has been defined to carry out certain tasks e.g. underscoring, saving data.

common business orientated language See **COBOL**.

communicating word processors Word processors connected via a network to allow very rapid office-to-office and/or business-to-business communication of text.

compatibility The ability of two devices whether hardware or software to work in conjunction, e.g. if a magnetic disk used on one computer can be read by another computer, the two computers are said to be compatible. Computer compatibility usually means software compatibility. If a program can be run on two computers without alteration to the program, the computers are said to be compatible.

compile To translate a high level computing language into a sequence of machine language instructions for the computer.

compiler (1) A program which compiles. (2) A program inside the computer which converts a program written in a high level language into a machine code version which can then be utilised by a computer.

compliment slips Small pieces of bond paper usually bearing the company logo and/or the same information as its letterheads which are used to accompany documents or other items in the post when a formal letter is not required.

complimentary close The phrase which closes a business or personal letter e.g. Yours faithfully, Yours sincerely, Kind regards, etc.

computer An electronic device which accepts information in the form of input data, puts it into storage and processes it according to instructions (or programs) and then outputs the result of that processing.

computer agencies Organisations specialising in the selection and recruitment of computer personnel for placement in employment. This service is usually free to the individual but there is a fee payable by the recruiting company or a percentage of a recruitee's salary.

computer aided design See **CAD.**

computer aided drawing The same as **computer aided design** although technically the term computer aided design is the more acceptable and commonly used of the two. See **CAD**.

computer aided instruction Refers to the use of computers as teaching machines. The computer presents instructional material and asks questions at a rate determined by the correctness of the student's responses, the questions being of increasing difficulty. If correct responses to questions are not given, the computer is programmed to give additional instructional material to the student. This method is also sometimes called 'programmed learning' as tuition is adapted to the needs of the individual students. Also known as **CAI**.

computer aided manufacture See **CAM**.

computer assisted instruction Usually known as **computer aided instruction**, involving the use of computers as teaching aids. Also known as **CAI**.

computer assisted/aided learning. Another name for **computer aided instruction**, involving the use of computers as teaching machines. Also known as **CAL**.

computer bureau A computer agency which runs other people's work on its own computer offering additional types of computing assistance and consultancy.

computer conferencing The interchange of messages on a particular topic over computer networks, e.g. electronic mail, teleconferencing.

computer originated microfilm See **COM**.

conditional page break A facility on most word processors that once the page length has been determined for a file, the word processor can be programmed to insert its own page break when, e.g. a paragraph is split with the last line appearing at the top of a new page. Instead, the word processor will automatically start a new page of printed type at the start of the paragraph in question. Conditional page breaking enables the operator to ensure that pages do not break in inconvenient places. Compare **unconditional page break**.

conference call A telephone network facility where several people may be connected to the same telephone call so that they all may take part in the same conversation or conference.

configuration The layout of the hardware in a particular computer system.

Confravision® A teleconferencing service offered by British Telecom. Two or three conference studios in different cities can be simultaneously inter-connected.

console The part of a data processing system which allows the operator to communicate with the computer, usually utilising a keyboard. Can also refer to the keyboard of an electronic switchboard e.g. PABX.

continuation sheet The second and subsequent pages of any document (letter, report, memorandum, etc.) and usually numbered chronologically.

continuous stationery A continuous piece of paper of three basic types: (1) *Rolls*, as used in teleprinters, of plain paper used in machines which are equipped with a cutting edge. (2) *Interfold* where forms are folded back and forward on each other at perforations in a concertina fashion. (3) *Fanfold* which usually refers to wide sheets of paper folded vertically several times in a concertina fashion and then folded horizontally at the separating perforations.

contrast The degree of luminance of a visual display unit and usually alterable or adjustable to the requirements of the individual by a switch on the VDU similar to that on a television screen.

control Generally refers to a control character whose occurence in a particular context will change a control operation on a computer. A typical example is a character which will initiate a carriage return.

control function The term applied to the controlling of equipment via a computer keyboard or joystick e.g. robots, remote control boats, remote control cars, etc.

control key A key on a computer keyboard which when depressed with a variety of other alpha keys gives additional facilities for the manipulation of files.

control program for microprocessors A commonly used operating system for computers. Also known as **CP/M**.

copy (1) The act of reading the contents of one magnetic disk and writing them to another. (2) The production of a likeness from an original using carbon paper, NCR paper or electronic equipment e.g. photocopier.

copy holder A piece of equipment which is used to hold text upright for ease in keying into a computer in a position near to the screen and keyboard and adjustable for the comfort of the operator.

copyright The author of any work holds the legal and exclusive right to reproduce that work unless he or she gives permission to another.

cordless telephone Literally a telephone without a cord connected to the telephone network and able to be used within a certain range of a telephone socket.

correctable film ribbon A white or transparent ribbon fitted across the printing point of a typewriter in a similar way to an inked ribbon, and operated via a key on the keyboard. When the key is depressed, the last printed character on the paper is deleted by being overtyped with the correctable ribbon. This allows for the new and correct character to be typed in its place. Often a feature of electronic typewriters.

correcting fluid Paper available in the form of a liquid which enables incorrect typing or writing to be painted over so that when dry, the new and correct version of text can be typed or written.

correcting thinner A liquid which when added to correcting fluid lengthens its life and prevents it from becoming too thick to be of effective use.

correction papers Narrow strips of paper coated with correcting chalk which can be inserted at the printing point of a typewriter. The original incorrect letter can be restruck and the impact of the correction paper will whiten it, so that the new and correct letter can be overtyped in its place.

corruption The unintended alteration or mutilation of computer data during processing, storage or transmission.

courier service A delivery and messenger service which is used for the speedy transportation of urgent documents between companies. Companies offering a courier service to industry and commerce often use motor cycle riders to avoid the delay which can be caused by traffic jams.

cpi Characters per inch. The number of characters to every horizontal inch of typing, usually 10, 12 or 15. Also known as **pitch**.

CP/M Control program for microprocessors. A widely used disc operating system for microcomputers.

cps Characters per second. The speed of a printer is measured by how many characters (letters, numbers or symbols) the printer can transfer to paper every second.

CPU Central processing unit. The part of a computer which contains the electronics for interpreting and executing computer programs, containing the ALU, core memory and the control unit which directs and controls the operation of the computer and its peripheral units.

crash When computer hardware or software malfunctions, or when a program which is running cannot be completed or re-started, a computer system is said to have crashed.

create The term given to the setting up of a new file in computing or word processing.

credit card call An organisation or company can be supplied by British Telecom with credit cards for use solely on the telephone. Credit card calls must be made via the operator, the credit card number quoted and the charge for the call will then be made direct to the company.

critical path analysis A mangement technique for planning complex operations so that they will be carried out in a proper sequence without incurring delays. Often a critical path analysis flowchart is used to depict the different series of operations allowing for progress to be monitored. Sometimes referred to as critical path method.

cross referencing A filing term used when it is deemed necessary to cross reference an index for files filed alphabetically, e.g. an invoice from North West Gas would be found under N. Familiarity may lead to a request for the Gas invoice. If a clerk looks under G for the file, he/she will not find it. Reference should then be made to the card index, where the cross reference would read something like 'Gas—see North West'

Crown copyright   The legal and exclusive right to material published by government departments. It is illegal to reproduce it without prior permission.

CRT   Cathode ray tube or cathode ray terminal. The acronym is sometimes used to refer to a complete cathode ray tube display unit. A television screen which displays text from a computer.

currency converter   A computer program enabling foreign transactions to be undertaken with the computer software being able to advise on exchange rates and fluctuation in exchange rates.

cursor   A marker on a VDU indicating the point at which text should be entered. Appearances can vary, some cursors are boxes, triangles or underlines, and some flash on and off.

custom designed software   Programs which have been specially designed or modified to meet the specific needs and requirements of a user.

cut and paste   A word processing term. Often an operator will find that the layout of text in a document needs to be changed. Instead of deleting and re-entering the text, the operator can mark the text to be repositioned (cut) and move it to a new location (paste). A labour-saving feature when large blocks of text have to be moved.

cycle   In computer terms, a complete sequence of operations at the end of which the series can be repeated.

Dd

daisy wheel The name given to a print where the type head is circular and the characters are attached round it on the ends of stalks.

daisy wheel printer A printer which makes use of a daisy wheel. The wheel rotates at speed until the required character is brought before a hammer. The character is then struck by the hammer against the ribbon. Daisy wheels are inter-changeable to facilitate different typefaces and produce letter-quality printout.

data Numbers or characters which provide the building blocks for information. Data is normally deemed to be input into a computer in order that information can be output.

data collection A general term for any means of gathering data for input to a computer usually associated with devices that can read badges, cards, tags, etc. and/or which have keyboards for inputting the data.

data processing Clerical, arithmetical and logical operations on data. In the context of information technology, data processing implies the use of a computer in its operations. Also known as **DP**.

Data Protection Act An Act of Parliament brought into effect to regulate computer data to protect the privacy of the individual.

database An organised collection of files of information that has been systematically recorded. The files can be inter-connected and form the base of an organisation's data processing system, with specific reference to information retrieval. If many people have access to one database through different terminals, it might then qualify to be called a databank.

Datapost®   A parcel and document delivery service offered by the Post Office, both nationally and internationally (the latter being called International Datapost). A door-to-door prompt delivery service is offered, packages being collected at agreed times from customers and delivered the next day.

Datel®   A contraction of **da**ta and **tel**ecommunications. A collective term for a group of data transmission systems where data may be sent from one data point or terminal to a central computer where it is processed and available for retrieval on demand. Data is converted into a suitable form for transmission by a modem.

Datel® services   The leased circuits offered by British Telecom which enable data to be transmitted over the telephone network. Several types of Datel services are offered, which vary according to the speed of transmission, sophistication of equipment, systems of retrieval and whether or not answering machines and automatic calling are required e.g. Datel 100, Datel 200 (useful where access to a computer is required by a number of low speed terminals, typically a time sharing bureau and its customers), Datel 2400, Datel 2412, Datel 48K, Datel 600.

dead file   When a file or record is no longer required, or is out of use or date, it is normally referred to as a dead file and is refiled in a dead filing system, for a period of time specified by the company, in case it has to be referred back to.

debtor   A person, company, organisation or commercial enterprise which owes a financial obligation.

debug   To test a computer program or routine and to isolate and correct errors to get rid of bugs or faults.

decimal filing   Also called the decimal filing classification system, it is a method of filing which breaks down the numerical sequence and can cover an infinite number of divisions and sub-divisions. Primary numbers i.e. 1, 2, 3 etc. are used for broad sections and within this range the decimal point denotes a sub-division, i.e. 1.1, 1.2, etc. Infinite sub-divisions within sub-divisions may follow, e.g. 1.11, 1.12, 1.13. This system is suitable where shelves of publications have to be catalogued and additions to existing groups may be made at any point between whole numbers. The decimal classification system referred to also as the Dewey classification system is often used in libraries.

decimal tab A facility of most word processors and some computers which when operated will line up columns of numbers so that the decimal points are aligned. When a decimal tab has been set, an operator can key in a numeric value which will be automatically aligned with other greater or smaller numerical values in that column, when the trigger character (the point or full stop) has been typed.

dedicated A program procedure, machine, network channel or system set apart for special use. Often the term is used to refer to word processors which will only do word processing i.e. they are dedicated to word processing.

deductions Amounts of money taken out of a wage or salary, usually for National Insurance, income tax, super-annuation and any voluntary deductions e.g. union sub-scription, savings scheme, holiday fund.

default The value of a variable which is used by a computer system, unless it is specifically altered by the keyboard to use another value.

default option The values controlling a computer's options that are pre-set and that will remain so, unless those values are changed by the user.

delete The removal of a word, phrase, line or block of text from a visual display unit screen or the removal of a file from a storage medium.

delivery time The time interval between the start of a transmission at an initiating terminal and the completion of reception at a receiving terminal.

density The amount of storage space on a magnetic disk.

designation   The title given to an individual as an employee of the organisation indicating that individual's position in the organisation e.g. Mr A Jones, Managing Director. The designation is normally typed below the signatory line in a business letter.

device   Physical parts of a computer system e.g. an output device may be a printer, an input device may be a keyboard and a storage device may be a magnetic disk.

Dewey decimal system   A particular form of decimal filing or decimal classification system in use in libraries. Also known as **decimal filing**.

diagnostic program   A program used in most computers to detect equipment malfunction.

dialling code booklet   A series of codes for Subscriber Trunk Dialling for the UK and for International Direct Dialling (overseas), operator services and call charges which comes in the form of a booklet or is printed at the front of the White pages telephone directory.

dialling tone   A continuous 'burr' when the telephone handset is lifted to indicate that the equipment is functioning and ready to accept an input telephone number.

dictating machine   There are three basic types of dictating machine; (1) the *dictation/transcription* machine which the dictator can use to make a recording and the typist can use to transcribe; (2) the *transcription* machine which can only be used by the audio typist to transcribe the cassette prepared at some other location; (3) the *portable* recorder which can be used in virtually any location as it is only pocket-sized and the tapes are sent to the audio typist who can then transcribe them on a different machine.

dictionary   A small, additional program available on some word processing packages which will check edited text for spelling errors against an inbuilt dictionary in the program. Ready made dictionaries can be purchased, many of which can be added to if the user requires the addition of specialised words.

digital   To do with numbers.

direct access   The ability to access data in a storage and retrieval system directly without having to scan any part of the storage file first. In a direct access system, each record's storage location is completely unconnected with any other record storage. Compare with **serial access**.

direct dialling in   Outside telephone callers may dial directly into a telephone extension, providing that they know the direct dialling number, without being answered by the switchboard. Also known as **direct inward dialling**.

direct inward dialling   A PABX facility which allows automatic direct routing for incoming telephone calls. Also known as **direct dialling in**.

direct process   A method of photocopying which uses paper which has been specially treated with a photoconductive coating. In the photocopier, the paper is given an electrostatic charge and then exposed to a light source, enabling an invisible charged image of the original to be retained on the paper. This image attracts fine particles of developer (either liquid or powder) and the image of the original appears on the paper. Sometimes called **electrofax** or **xerography**. Compare with **indirect process**.

directory   A computer record which informs the operating system of the whereabouts of a file which is held in the backing storage.

directory enquiries   A British Telecom service which provides details of telephone numbers provided the caller can specify the correct name and address.

discriminatory call-barring   Telephone extensions to a telephone network switchboard may be barred from certain areas of use e.g. from Subscriber Trunk Dialling or International Direct Dialling. Also known as **barred extensions**.

disk A flat circular medium used for magnetic backing storage of information and programs. A disk is divided into recording tracks and sub-divided into sectors. Each track and sector is addressable which gives disk storage its random access capability, enabling programs and data to be accessed or retrieved quickly.

disk box A plastic box which will house usually ten floppy disks and which will protect them from contamination by dust. A box is sufficiently safe storage for transporting the disk to various locations.

disk capacity The amount of storage space on a disk.

disk drive An electro-mechanical device which houses a magnetic disk effecting necessary movement and writing to or reading from the disk.

disk operating system Software that manages the storage and retrieval of information on disk and controls the operation of all activities relating to the use of magnetic disks in a computer system. Also known as **DOS**.

diskette A magnetic or floppy disk.

display (1) The production of a visual record on a television (or similar) screen, the term being sometimes used to apply to the screen itself.   (2) The layout of a document (letter, memorandum, etc.) in the form of fully blocked, semi blocked or indented display.

distributed logic Computer systems where logic or intelligence are distributed in the system rather than located centrally e.g. some word processing systems link intelligent terminals which may make shared use of other resources such as storage, printer.

document (1) A medium and the data recorded on it. Most commonly refers to print on paper.   (2) A generic term in business used to refer to any documentation printed for and used by an organisation which usually bears the name and address of that organisation e.g. letterhead, memorandum, invoice, quotation, estimate, delivery note, order, statement, etc.

document merge   A facility of most word processors to join together two separate documents making one final document. If more than two documents are integrated, the process is referred to as document assembly.

document shredder   A machine used in offices into which disused but confidential documents can be fed and which shreds them into tiny pieces so that the reading of the output is impossible.

document based system   A word processing program where each file is produced as a whole document and not divided on screen into pages. Often the only way to see where pages will break is to print a draft of the file and then to edit the file, enforcing more suitable page breaks if required. It is common on a document based system to find a word count facility. Compare **page based system**.

documentation   Program specifications, operating instructions and manuals, printed versions of software programs and diagrams of hardware and anything else in print about a computer system which can be used to guide the service staff in operation, repair or familiarisation.

dongle   A memory chip containing software specially packaged so that it can be plugged directly into a microcomputer in order that the software contained on the memory chip can be utilised by the operator. Also known as **cartridge**.

DOS   Disk operating system. Software that manages the storage and retrieval of information on disk.

dot matrix printer   A printer capable of producing work at high speed which uses a series of electrically hammered moving pins to create characters made up of a pattern of dots. Printed output material is not considered to be of letter quality.

double density disk   A magnetic disk with twice the storage capacity of a standard disk of the same dimension. Also known as **dual density disk**.

down In computing terms, a system is said to be down when it is not operating.

download The transference of data or programs from one computer to another e.g. from a mainframe to a micro-computer.

downtime A period when computer equipment is not operating because of malfunction, maintenance, etc.

DP Data processing. Clerical, arithmetical and logical operations on data. Data processing in the context of information technology implies the use of a computer in its operations.

draft The first rough copy of a document usually typed with wide left and right margins in double line spacing so that handwritten corrections and comments may be made if required.

drive A electronic device used to load a disk onto a computer system.

drum printer A type of line printer which prints from a drum engraved with identical characters in each print position across the drum, with a full set of characters engraved in each print position around the drum.

dual density disk See **double density disk**.

dual pitch printer A printer which has the facility to switch from one type size to another by the movement of a switch. Type sizes offered are normally 10 or 12 characters to the inch, although some printers offer an additional 15 characters to the inch.

dual spectrum A method of photocopying which produces a negative first by exposing the original document and the sensitised side of special paper to a light source. The negative is then used by the machine to produce the finished copy similar to a photograph. This process allows for colour copying.

dual purpose dictating machine   A machine used in audio typing which can be used both for dictation by the author and also by the typist for transcribing the text.

dumb terminal   Input or output terminals from a central computer which have no independent processing capability of their own. Operations can only be carried out and information processed when the terminal is connected to a computer. Compare with **intelligent terminal** or **smart terminal**.

dump   The transfer of data from one computer storage area to another or, more usually, to output.

dumping   The copying of contents of a storage area onto another medium usually for the purpose of security or checking.

duplicate   To make one or more copies of an original document, using spirit, stencil (or ink), or off-set litho duplicators.

duplicator   A generic term which identifies one of the following: spirit duplicator, stencil (or ink) duplicator or off-set litho duplicator, all of which are used in the reproduction of multiple copy documents.

Ee

EAPROM   Electrically alterable programmable read only memory. Read only memory which can be erased by passing an electrical current through it and then re-used or re-programmed.

EAROM   Electrically alterable read only memory. Read only memory which can be erased by passing an electrical current through it and then re-used i.e. new data entered. Also known as electrically erasable read only memory or **EEROM**.

edge punched cards   A filing system. The cards have small holes around the edges, each hole relating to a particular item of information. At selected places the holes are converted into slots by means of a special punch. When cards are stacked and a needle is pushed through the pack at any given point, all cards which have been slotted and contain the required information will drop clear and can be removed. This enables cards to be replaced in random order.

edit   The process of removing or inserting information by an operator when a record is passed through a computer.

electric typewriter   Similar in every feature to a manual typewriter except that with the use of an electric motor, an automatic carriage return is enabled, together with letter repetition. Type pressure is consistent and printed text often has a much better appearance.

electrically alterable read only memory   See **EAROM**.

electrofax   Another name for fax or facsimile transmission. A system which can transmit a representation of the form and content of a document over a telecommunications link.

electronic diary An ability of electronic mail to store diaries and interrogate them to arrange meetings. All involved employees of a company key in their planned appointments for as far in advance as they are booked. Diaries are electronically checked when meetings have to be arranged to ensure that all employees are available. Users concerned will see when appointments have been made when checking their diaries.

electronic in tray A term referring to the reception of documents transmitted by electronic mail.

electronic mail The electronic transmission and distribution of messages permitting communication between two or more parties using electronic technology. Computerised information is sent over satellites, cables or telephone wires.

electronic stencil cutter A machine capable of cutting a stencil from an original document, the stencil to be used on an ink duplicator. An advantage of preparing a master stencil by the use of an electronic stencil cutter is that all details on the original document will be cut, including drawings and letterhead designs.

electronic switching system A digital telephone switching system which provides special services such as speed dialling, call transfer and three way calling.

electronic typewriter Similar in many ways to an electric typewriter but offering additional facilities such as multi-pitch selection, often including proportional spacing, back space correction key with varying memory capacity, fast back key to take the operator back to the start of a line, automatic paper insertion, automatic tabulation setting, automatic decimal tabulation, automatic centring, right hand margin justification, automatic underscore and indent, and emboldening facility.

electrostatic copier A machine which produces exact copies of original documents at the touch of a button. There is no requirement for masters to be prepared beforehand nor for a specialist operator. Sophisticated electrostatic copiers can produce thousands of copies at high speed, turn copies over to print on the other side and collate the copies for distribution. Most electrostatic copies can produce transparencies for overhead projectors and off-set plates.

electrostatic printer   A non-impact printer which produces electrostatic charges on paper in the design to be copied. A toner is attracted to the charged area which then becomes visible and which is fused to the paper using a heat process. Also known as **xerography**.

elite   A measurement of type, namely twelve characters to every horizontal inch of typescript.

embolden   A technique used by impact printers to produce bold type which gives a thicker and darker impression by repeated striking of the letters and is usually used for emphasis, e.g. headings.

emergency services   A telephone network service obtained by dialling 999 which should be used in emergency only. The services offered are fire, police, ambulance and coastguard.

emulator   Hardware or software which makes a computer system appear to other hardware or software as another system, e.g. a word processor may be able to emulate a telex or one particular type of computer may be able to appear to software as a different type of computer.

enclosures   Any documents, copy documents, cheques, maps, diagrams, etc. that are sent through the post accompanying a letter. It is usual practice for the word *Enc* or *Encs* to appear in the bottom left hand corner of the accompanying letter, in the event that the letter and contents become separated when opened.

end pages   Videotext pages which contain information and distinct from those pages which aid the user in locating this information.

end user   In information technology a term used to describe the individual who operates a computer system.

engaged tone A series of high pitched 'beeps' on a telephone line which signifies that the line dialled is currently in use.

enter A key on a computer keyboard which is used to signify to the computer that data which has just been typed to the screen or VDU is ready for input. As most input data will not be accepted until the enter key has been struck, a facility for immediate error correction is maintained.

EPROM Erasable programmable read only memory. A chip containing a program which it will hold until it is erased by exposing the surface of the chip to ultra violet light. The chip has the facility to be reprogrammed.

erasable programmable read only memory See **EPROM**.

erasable read only memory See **EROM**.

ergonomics The study and analysis of how people and machines work together.

EROM Erasable read only memory. A chip containing a computer program which will hold it until it is erased by exposing the surface of the chip to ultra violet light.

esc Short for *escape* and a function key appearing on a computer keyboard.

escape Escape character or a character in a computer data string which leads to an exit from a code. Also known as **esc** and usually denoted as such on a computer keyboard.

ex-directory Telephone numbers which do not appear in the printed local White pages directories. These numbers generally apply to private telephone lines.

expanding files A lightweight cardboard-box type file, usually alphabetically sectioned with a concertina'd base. The fuller the file becomes, the more the concertina base will expand, thus creating more filing room as and when needed.

express delivery   A postal service which ensures speedy delivery of parcels and mail for which a fee in addition to normal postal rates is payable. Express delivery is only available for items addresses to places in the Channel Islands, Isle of Man and Irish Republic.

extension   The name given to a telephone connected to a switchboard console which in turn is connected to the telephone network.

extension metering   A metering system which records the number of units used by each extension of a PABX switchboard, usually found in hotels where guests may dial their own calls and have them charged to their account. Also known as **call metering**.

external storage   Any storage medium which is portable e.g. magnetic disks. Compare **internal storage**.

Ff

facsimile transceiver   The name given to a system which can transmit and receive a representation of the form and content of documents over a telecommunications link. The usual term is **facsimile transmission**.

facsimile transmission   A system which can transmit a representation of the form and content of documents over a telecommunications link where the recipient receives a complete copy of the original document, not just its information contents. Receiving and sending facsimile transmission terminals must be compatible, so standardisation is particularly important. Also known as **fax**.

fax   Abbreviation for **facsimile transmission** or facsimile communication.

feedback   The return of a part of the output from a computer system to its input so as to control the output to within pre-determined limits, when those limits have been over-ridden.

fibre optics   Very fine glass threads bundled together as cables and allowing telecommunications to occur by pulsing light. Also known as **optical fibre**.

fiche   A frame of microfilm which is used for storage information. Also known as **microfiche**.

field   A section of a computer record designated for the storage of specific information. A fixed field has a defined, unvarying length, whereas a variable field can be assigned different length values.

field length   The length of a section of a computer record which has been designated for the storage of specific information. Length can be fixed or variable.

fifth generation computer The coming generation of computers with greatly increased processing power which facilitates the running of user-friendly artificial intelligence software.

file An organised and structured collection of information recorded as a unit with an identifying name e.g. a computer program can be a file.

filename A series of characters used to identify a file.

firmware A computer program written into a storage medium from which it cannot be accidentally erased. Firmware is often stored in read only memory (ROM) which is designed so that files cannot be overwritten. The term also applies to the electronic devices containing such a program.

first class post A Post Office service for inland surface mail which ensures that letters are delivered the next day if posted before twelve noon on the previous day.

fixed head Read/write heads in a central processing unit or disk drive which are kept stationary.

fixed head disk A disk memory with one read/write head for track on the disk.

fixed time call A British Telecom service available through the operator on the telephone network. The caller books a call (usually long distance, although not necessarily) via the operator for a certain time. The operator will log the call and connect both lines at the given time.

flag Information which can be added to computer data in order to characterise the data or to provide information about it. Sometimes called a marker, point or a tag.

flimsy In typewriting, a flimsy refers to a carbon copy made of any typewritten material made on bank paper which is very thin.

floppy disk   A thin disk made of a flexible material with one or both sides coated to accept magnetic recording. Floppy disks are usually either 5¼ inches or 8 inches in diameter. Also known as **magnetic disk**.

flowchart   A graphical representation showing the sequence of events and choices which need to be made in the solution of a problem, using symbolic shapes such as rectangles and diamonds and usually, although not exclusively, relating to a computer program.

flowcharting   A method of representing a series of events by means of lines linking symbols. The lines represent inter-connection and the symbols represent events or processes. Systems flowcharts represent the relationship between events in a data processing system. Program flowcharts show the logical components of a computer program.

follow-up file   A method of controlling the whereabouts of files in a manual filing system. 'Out' cards are inserted in the place of folders when they are withdrawn from the filing system, bearing the name of the person who has taken the folder and the date it was taken. As the file is returned, the 'out' card is withdrawn and the name and date deleted. Any missing file therefore which is needed urgently can easily be 'followed up'.

font   A set of characters and numbers of one shape, style and size of type. Also known as **fount** (font is the US spelling).

footer   Usually a feature of word processing programs, a footer can be typed in at the beginning of a file using a special command and will be printed at the foot of each page within that file.

forecast   Specifically an accounting term and a facility of spreadsheet software, that given past information of e.g. sales turnover over five previous years, the program can work out the percentage growth and estimate the following year's sales on that percentage automatically.

foreground   A facility of some computers whereby high priority tasks can be carried out whilst those of low priority are also being carried out in the background, e.g. a printer may be printing in background while the operator is editing in foreground.

form documents   Standard letters used by an organisation which will answer correspondence of a similar nature giving the same information to all correspondents. Also known as **form letters**.

form feed   A mechanical device which positions, repositions and advances paper in a printer.

form feeder   A mechanism that feeds stacks of single sheet paper into a printer.

form letter   A standard letter produced in multiple copies by a word processor with names and addresses of recipients keyed in one at a time or automatically accessed from a word processing mailing list i.e. a standard letter merged with variable information.

format   (1) To format is to arrange data or text according to specific instructions.   (2) An arrangement of data. It may refer to the layout of a printed document, the order of instructions in a program or the arrangement of data in a computer file.

formula   A computing term used in spreadsheet software. If several columns of figures have to be totalled, or a percentage of each calculated, a formula can be set up to do this and then run. The calculations for each column will then take place automatically and simultaneously rather than totalling and calculating each column individually.

FORTRAN   Formula translator. A high level computer programming language used specifically for scientific, technical or mathematical applications.

fount   A set of characters and numbers of one shape, style and size of type. Also known as **font** which is the US spelling.

fourth generation computers The majority of contemporary computers.

franking machine A machine which, when letters for posting are passed through it, will stamp them with the date and the pre-set postage value. Mainly a labour-saving device avoiding the sticking of stamps onto letters and useful in large organisations. Company logos can also appear on the franking. Machines can be credited at Post Offices.

Freefone® A British Telecom facility available via the telephone network. When companies offer a telephone number to ring as Freefone XXXX, the customer can dial the operator, quote the Freefone number and be connected to that company at no personal charge. The organisation who are offering the Freefone number are then charged for the price of the call, plus a fee for the facility. The service is used to encourage people to contact business and industry.

Freepost® A Post Office service. When companies offer a Freepost mailing address, the sender of the letter does not need to use a stamp on that letter, providing the word Freepost appears in the address. The recipient of the letter is then charged for the cost of mailing the letter, plus a fee for the facility. The service is used to encourage people to contact business and industry.

friction fed A term which refers to the action of paper passing through a printer. In friction fed printers, the pressure of the roller and the platen draw the paper through the printer, without the need for a special mechanism. Compare **tractor fed**.

full punctuation The term full punctuation refers generally to business documents. If full punctuation is used, all address lines end with a comma, initials have full stops after them, etc. For example:

> Mr. A. Jones,
> 42, Whitworth Road,
> Shoreham.

full size display A visual display unit screen capable of showing a full A4 size document, giving the operator some indication of how the printed output will look. Most VDU screens display approximately half a page.

fully blocked letters A typing term referring to the layout of business letters where all lines of type commence at the left hand margin, including the reference and address, although sometimes the date appears to the right hand side for ease in filing.

function key One or more keys on a computer keyboard which allows a user to issue a series of commands with one key depression, provided that the keys have been allocated special functions. Function keys can either be defined by the user or be already programmed into purpose-built terminals.

Gg

garbage in garbage out   A computing term meaning that the quality of information you get out is only as good as the quality of information put in, i.e. incorrect output results from incorrect input. Also known as **GIGO**.

geographical filing   A filing classification system where files are kept according to geographical district and although of limited application, a system which can be useful in sales and transport departments of companies. It is usual for files in each division to be held alphabetically.

GIGO   Garbage in, garbage out. A computing term, meaning incorrect output resulting from incorrect input.

glare   The word given to the excessive amount of luminance emitted from a visual display unit screen. Most computers have a switch facility which will alter the degree of luminance. Glare is also sometimes caused by light from windows or lamps reflecting off a terminal.

global search   A word processing feature which activates the cursor to find every occurrence of a pre-determined character, word or phrase in a file.

global search and replace   An editing function in word processing where the cursor will search for each occurrence of a particular character, word or phrase and replace each occurrence with another pre-determined character, word or phrase. Also know as **search and replace.**

golfball   The popular description of the spherical typehead found on the IBM electric typewriter.

GRACE   Group routing and charging equipment. Telephone calls made via STD are charged by this system.

grafting The correction of a large section of a stencil by the cutting of a hole in the stencil to remove the error and the replacement of the hole by a slightly larger piece of new stencil onto which the correction has been typed, the new piece of stencil being glued to the original using stencil correcting fluid.

graphics A generic term referring to the appearance of pictures or diagrams on a VDU as a result of data processing.

graphics plotter A device similar to a printer which provides hard copy output of computer graphics displayed on a screen. There are two main types: drum and flatbed.

gross In gross pay, the amount of salary or wage earned each month or week, before the deduction of income tax, National Insurance, superannuation and other voluntary deductions.

group calling Used with operator connected extensions, incoming telephone calls can automatically be re-routed to other extensions in a pre-determined order until the call has been taken. This facility may also be available from internal extensions. Also known as group hunting.

group routing and charging equipment See **GRACE**.

guide cards The first card of a card index file giving an easy reference to where individual cards may be found. Alphabetical classification is the most popular form of indexing on a guide card.

guillotine A piece of office equipment similar in principle to the original Guillotine but which is used to neatly cut paper and card.

Hh

handshaking   The exchange of signals between two pieces of equipment, one of which is transmitting and the other receiving, prior to the establishment of full transmission between the two.

hard copy   Permanent output from a computer and usually synonymous with print on paper.

hard disk   A magnetic disk hermetically sealed to prevent contamination by dust and moisture. Hard disks offer large storage capacity and are used for the bulk storage of computer data. Mainframe computers use hard disks. The alternative name rigid disk is sometimes used.

hard sectoring   The marking of sector boundaries on a magnetic disk by the punching of holes in the disk. All available space can be used for data storage. Contrast with **soft sectoring**.

hardware   The magnetic, electrical, mechanical and electronic components which make up a computer.

head   A device which reads and records or erases information on a computer storage medium.

header   A word processing facility which allows the operator to type a line of information at the top of a file and for that line of information to be printed at the top of each page as the file is printed.

heat transfer copier   A photocopying process which uses heat instead of light to form the copy image using a special heat-sensitive copy paper. Original images must have a carbon or metallic content. This method is also known as thermal copying.

help menu A facility of many computers and word processors which enables the user to find information on available commands and their syntax without leaving the program in use and without having to refer to the manual.

hexidecimal code A data code which uses the base 16 as compared with base 2 for binary code and base 10 for decimal code.

high level language A computer programming language which allows a user to employ instructions close to his/her own familiar language rather than machine code. The higher the level of the language, the nearer the language is to English language. The most common high level languages are ALGOL, COBOL, BASIC, FORTRAN and PASCAL.

high resolution The fineness of detail distinguishable in an image and often referred to the screen of a visual display unit.

hold A facility available on a PABX switchboard which the operator can use to hold the incoming call whilst checking with the extension user whether or not he/she wishes to take the call. Sometimes referred to as hold for enquiry.

home The starting point for a cursor on the screen of a visual display unit, i.e. page one, line one, column one.

hot zone An area adjacent to and to the left of the right hand margin on a word processor. This area is adjustable in width so that any word starting in the hot zone which may exceed the pre-determined line length may be hyphenated by the user, or overrun to the beginning of a new line.

housekeeping Routine maintenance of computer programs which contributes overall to the efficiency of a computer's usage.

hybrid system A computer system combining analogue and digital devices e.g. in the supply of electricity, signals can come from power stations, the information assembled into meaning form which are injected into the analogue computer. In the event e.g. of a power failure, output from the analogue computer can be processed by the digital computer and typed hard copy output is produced, giving notification where the power failure has occurred.

Ii

icon An image on the screen of an advanced micro-computer resembling a familiar office object, e.g. document, tray, and representing a work area in the computer. The work area is accessed by moving the cursor to the icon and then pressing a key to call up that work area. Areas are sometimes accessed using a mouse.

IDD International direct distance dialling. Numeric area codes used in the connection of international calls on the telephone network.

idle time Time during which a machine is ready for operation but is not in actual use.

image printer Using optical technology, a printer which will compose an image of a complete page from digital input, the final copy being produced as print on paper.

immediate access store A storage area in a computer into which information can be written and from which it can be instantly read no matter where it is in the store. Often referred to as **random access memory**.

impact printing A means of printing where the characters are formed on the paper by means of a hammer striking the ribbon e.g. dot matrix printers, line printers.

income tax A statutory deduction. Every employee has a statutory duty to pay income tax on his/her wage or salary. The amount is normally deducted by the employer and forwarded to the Collector of Taxes at monthly intervals. All employees are entitled to an amount of tax-free pay which is available once an employee has been allotted a tax code number from his/her local tax office.

incompatibility If a program capable of running on one computer cannot be run on another computer, the software is said to be incompatible. Compare with **compatibility**.

indent The movement in of text from the left hand margin, usually at the beginning of a paragraph and half an inch, i.e. six character spaces for elite type and five for pica typescript.

index A series of headings which identify and characterise a document or other piece of information, which can be arranged in a variety of ways to suit the user's needs. Most indices (plural) are in alphabetical order. Examples are indices of book contents appearing at the back of books.

indexing (1) The method of identifying where classified material can be found. Some methods of filing are self-indexing e.g. dictionary, telephone directory. (2) In word processing, an index can be automatically created by the software, provided that compiling entries are flagged in the original text. This is used sometimes for the setting up of a contents page.

indirect process Refers to the method of photocopying, as in plain paper copiers, where a photoconductive coating is formed of the original document inside the photocopying unit. This image is then transferred to an ordinary sheet of paper which undergoes a heating process to make it into a permanent copy.

information Data processed and put together in a meaningful form.

information technology By means of computers and telecommunications, vocal, pictorial, textual and numerical information is acquired, processed, stored and disseminated.

in house A communications network which is contained in one set of buildings.

initialise The defining of initial values of variables at the start of a program's execution.

ink duplicator Sometimes referred to as a stencil duplicator, a machine which can give 5000 or more good copies from a single master stencil which has been prepared by hand, typewriter, electronic stencil cutter or thermal photocopier.

ink jet printer A printer controlled by digitally stored information whose main feature is that each copy can differ, as the printing is individually controlled. Each character is generated by a drop of liquid which is vibrated, a charge passed through it and then deflected by electrostatic fields. The deflection is varied so that the ink drops are directed to specific parts of the paper sheet.

input The putting in of information to a computer by an operator from a keyboard and therefore being information received by a computer.

input device A piece of equipment which allows data and instructions to be entered into a computer's memory, e.g. keyboard, terminal, light pen, MICR, OCR.

insert The addition of a word, phrase or paragraph to any text that has already been produced.

insert mode Any text that is typed at a computer keyboard which is added to the version which already appears on the visual display unit. Contrast with **overwrite mode**.

integrated In reference to computer packages, sometimes called a suite, the linking together of a database, spreadsheet, word processing and graphics which can interact actively, e.g. where the operator can copy the spreadsheet results into a report prepared within word processing.

integrated circuit A piece of silicon etched with tiny electronic circuits usually between one and five centimetres in length. The type normally found in computers is called a logic chip. Also known as **chip**.

integrated packages   Computer software purchased as one package in which filing (database), spreadsheet and word processing programs are linked together. Many integrated packages also link with a graphics program to give visual representation; sometimes referred to as a suite of programs.

Integrated Services Digital Network   A network carrying digital information which can combine voice and data in the same channels providing a wide range of communication options.

intelligent terminal   A computer terminal which can be used to process data on its own without the help of a central processor to which it may be connected.

Intelpost®   An electronic letter service allowing users of the Post Office to send documents around the country having them delivered within hours. The service is intended for customers who do not have their own facsimile transmission service.

interactive   A method of operating the computer where the user is in direct and continual communication with the computer and the computer is in direct and continual communication with the operator.

interactive video   An electronic system that makes computer based information available via a VDU and where the information is carried from the computer to the receiver by cable, usually telephone lines. A UK form of interactive video is Prestel, where instead of passively receiving information, users can interact individually with the computer.

intercom   A device enabling communication to take place between two or more locations without the need for going through the main telephone system or switchboard. An intercom unit provides a useful communication link between offices.

interface   The connecting link between two parts of a computer system, e.g. the cable that runs between a word processing terminal and its disk drive.

internal communication This is often a computerised method in which messages are transferred from one user to the file of another to await collection.

internal storage The internal read only memory of a computer where programs and data are stored.

International Datel® A British Telecom service enabling data to be transmitted over the telephone network or leased circuits internationally. Datel 200, 600 and 2400 services provide for the transmission of data to most of Europe, the US and several other countries.

International Packet Switching Service A public automatic switched data service providing access between UK data terminals and computer systems abroad and vice versa. Also known as **IPSS**.

International Telegrams A Post Office facility which offers the same day delivery of a message internationally. Messages may be handed in at a Post Office, sent by telex or dictated by telephone call.

interpreter If a computer program has not been previously compiled or assembled, an interpreter program can control the execution of the first program.

IT Information technology.

inventory A list of items in stock at the time of taking the list, eased if stock has been computerised since the stock position can be printed out at any time with such information as the total costing of all items in cost and stock re-order lists.

invoice A document made out whenever one person sells goods to another constituting a contract for the sale of goods. Invoices often have as many as five copies printed on different coloured papers for ease of recognition and internal handling.

IPSS International Packet Switching Service.

Jj

justified text   Text which has an even right margin equal to the left margin and where the right hand margin appears vertically straight. Some word processors will justify text as a default; others print ragged right as a default. It is usually not difficult to switch to and from justified text.

justify   To adjust the positions of words on a page, distributing additional space in lines so that the right margin forms a straight vertical and parallel edge to the left margin.

Kk

key (1) A button which is depressed or touched to register a character. (2) In filing a group of characters used in the identification of an item to allow access to it as in numerical filing.

keyboard An input device for a computer usually alphanumeric but also containing special keys which perform particular functions and which is manually operated to input data or instructions.

key entry The entry of standardised information on the keys of a computer terminal. An activity usually associated with data processing and often repetitive.

keypad A hand-held keyboard which provides electronic input to a computer having fewer keys than a normal computer keyboard.

key punch A device which perforates cards in specified locations by a user at a keyboard. Also known as **card punch**.

keypunch operator A person who operates punched card or punched tape whose pay is usually based on quantity of output.

keytape The recording of data directly onto a magnetic tape without the use of any other medium.

key-to-tape A method for entering data in which that data is sent directly from a keyboard to a magnetic tape based file.

KHz Short for kilohertz, one thousand hertz. A unit of measurement.

Ll

LAM   Laser accessed memory. Similar in theory to random access memory, but much quicker.

LAN   Local area network. A system which links together computers, electronic mail, word processors and other electronic office equipment to form an inter-office network.

laser   An acronym for light amplification by the simulated emission of radiation. A device emitting a powerful pure light producing a narrow light beam which can be used for a range of communication activities, e.g. printing, optical scanning. A laser beam can also be used to carry signals along optical fibres.

laser accessed memory   See **LAM**.

laser disk   A form of video used to access information held on a disk rather than on a tape. The disk is read by decoding patterns produced by a laser light reflected off the disk's surface.

laser printer   A printer using a laser light source to write on paper which is then passed through an ink powder. Ink is attracted to the area on the paper which has been written on and excess powder is removed. The ink is then fixed by chemical treatment or heat. Laser printers are known to give high quality output at very fast rates, e.g. 2000 pages per minute, and have the additional facility to be able to print form headings at the same time as information, so that pre-printed stationery is not required. Also known as **laser writer**.

laser writer   A printer capable of producing documents in seconds that are printed so perfectly that the words look typeset. Also known as **laser printer**.

lateral filing   Refers to filing equipment and the storage of material on shelves, in cupboards or on racks. Files are laid on their spines usually in suspended pockets with the end of each file in view bearing the index strip upon it. A large number of files can therefore be seen at any one time. Valuable floor space is saved as it is possible to store records virtually from floor to ceiling.

layout   The design of a letter, form or environment. Also known as **format**.

LCD   Liquid crystal display. Liquid crystals that can be switched from an opaque to a transparent state providing a data display if the liquid crystals are interposed between a light source and the observer.

letter opening machine   A piece of equipment found in the mail room of companies used to aid the process of opening bulk mail.

letter quality   The term usually refers to output from a printer where the printing is indistinguishable from that typed on a good electric typewriter and acceptable for distribution outside an organisation.

letter quality printer   Any printer that can produce print of the same quality as a good electric typewriter.

letterhead   A piece of bond A4 or A5 paper bearing the name, address and telephone number of a company, usually a company logo and sometimes the names of directors and the VAT registration number. Letterheads are used for all communication outside a company.

light pen   A device shaped like a pen used in conjunction with a visual display unit which when moved over the screen allows the user to communicate directly with a computer. Often used for drawing in graphics software.

line feed A facility of most printers to automatically move the paper up through the printing mechanism one line at a time. This is achieved either by pressing a button (line feed button) on the printer itself, or via the software in use at the time.

line length The number of characters printed horizontally across one line of a page between the left and the right hand margins. It is usual in word processing that the line length of a document be specified within the computer file either by specifying the line length itself, or by the setting of the left and right margins which will set the line length by default.

line printer A device for printing computer output producing text one line at a time. Sets of characters on continuous belts are contained within the printer. As paper is fed past the printing head, an entire line of characters is printed. Sometimes known as line at a time printers.

line spacing The number of lines of space which appear between each typed line of text and added to the line of text for counting purposes e.g. single line spacing is one line of text with no space between it and the next line of text (1 line of text + 0 lines of space = single spacing). Double line spacing is one line of text with one line of space before the next line of text (1 line of text + 1 line of space = double line spacing) etc.

line status (1) A message from the computer to the user indicating whether or not it is ready to receive or transmit. (2) A line of information shown on a VDU giving the operator the status of the cursor at any time i.e. the line number, column number and page number.

lines per minute See **lpm**.

liquid crystal display Liquid crystals can be switched from an opaque to a transparent state when interposed between a light source and an observer. Liquid crystal display is often used on calculators. Also known as **LCD**.

list (1) An ordered set of items of data. (2) An ordered set of records within a file. (3) The action of printing or displaying a list within a file without performing an additional processing on a computer.

load To enter information or a program into a computer from a storage device.

local area network A private system connecting devices within a small area, which links together computers, electronic mail, word processors and other electronic office equipment to give an inter-office or inter-site network. Networks can also be given access to external networks e.g. public telephone and data transmission network, viewdata, information retrieval systems, etc.

local calls Calls made over the telephone network within a certain radius (less than 56 kilometres) of the equipment being used and charged at a cheaper rate than national calls which are calls outside the 56 kilometres radius.

location Designated by a specific address, a place in a computer's memory where information is stored.

log A device connected to PABX switchboards which produces a report giving details of all telephone calls made on each extension to the switchboard, including date, number called, town/country called, time, duration and cost.

logging off The termination of a session on a computer.

logging on The starting up of a session on a computer for which a password is often required.

logo A graphical representation of a company's or organisation's name sometimes incorporating the field of industry, commerce or interest in which that company is involved, becoming known as the company's trademark. Sometimes referred to as logotype.

LOGO A high level interactive computing language most frequently used in educational applications.

log on/off   To initiate or terminate on-line interaction with a computer.

loop   A series of instructions within a computer program which are performed continuously until a condition which has been pre-determined is met, when the computer will exit from the loop and carry on with the next instruction in the original program.

loose leaf index books   A method of filing using loose leaf binders with sets of pages separated by guide sheets. Sheets are easily inserted and removed when changes to information take place. Loose leaf index books are often used for catalogues where specifications are subject to change.

loudspeaker   Connected to a public address system, loud-speakers are generally placed in different positions on the company's premises. Announcements can be made via the loudspeaker to locate members of staff, using a microphone and amplifier system in the telephone office.

low level language   A computer language which is very close to the computer's own machine code. Each low level language instruction has its own direct machine code equivalent.

lower case   Small letters of a fount, e.g. a as opposed to A.

lpm   Lines per minute. The speed at which printers produce hard copy output.

luminance   The brightness of a television screen or a visual display unit, adjustable by the use of the luminance control button to suit the needs of the individual operator.

Mm

machine code A binary code used in machine language for a machine's basic instructions which are directly acceptable to the central processing unit of a computer system.

machine language A language used by a computer for internal communications with its related parts and the language in which a computer performs arithmetic and editing functions.

macro An abbreviation for macro code. An instructional code which permits single words to generate several computer instructions.

magnetic bubble memory A type of storage in which information is encoded onto a thin film of magnetic silicate in the form of bubbles detected by a special sensor which will emit an electronic pulse as each bubble passes the read head.

magnetic card A piece of cardboard or plastic with a magnetisable surface on which data can be recorded.

magnetic disk A circular sheet of material coated with a magnetic oxide and used as a form of backing storage. Also known as **disk**.

magnetic drum A form of backing storage giving rapid direct access and large storage capacity. The drum is cylindrical having a magnetisable surface containing a number of recording tracks, which is rotated very quickly as several read/write heads search for and access data with high transfer rates.

magnetic ink character recognition Numbers printed in

magnetic ink which can be read visually and by a computer's MICR reader, e.g. numbers which are printed across the bottom of bank cheques. Also known as **MICR**.

magnetic tape   Plastic tape coated with a magnetic oxide which allows data to be entered and accessed by means of read/write heads passed which the tape is wound, from one reel to another. All entries and searches have to be carried out sequentially.

mail box   A name for electronic mail or a system in which computer messages are transferred from one user to the file of another, and often applied to systems based on interactive videotex.

mail log   A computerised method of internal communication.

mail merge   The process of combining a document file and a mailing list in word processing for the production of a standard letter. A document file containing the text of the communication is integrated with a file listing the names and addresses of all clients, customers and companies who are to receive the letter giving an output where one letter is printed for each address, with the appearance of an originally typed letter. Mail merge software is often used in marketing and product promotion environments.

mailing list   A computer file holding the names and addresses of all companies and businesses with whom the master company may correspond.

mainframe   The central processing unit of a large computer installation with many terminals attached and distinguishing the computer from a minicomputer or microcomputer.

mainstore   A computer's memory capable of storing information temporarily or permanently. Also known as **memory**.

management information system A system involving a computer which provides information for decision-making in the control and development of a business e.g. inventory levels, absenteeism, external product prices.

manual typewriter Referred to also as a standard typewriter, a machine where the typist's fingers provide the power to operate typebars and a mechanism producing movement of a carriage and eventually print on paper. A machine of this type has an 11 or 13 inch carriage and offers either pica or elite typescript.

margin The space which appears between the left hand edge of the paper and the start of the typed text, or the space which appears between the last typed letter of text on a line and the right hand edge of the paper, referred to as left or right margin.

mark To identify by a symbol or control key the beginning and end of a line or block of text usually for movement, copying or deletion.

marker A non-printing character which can identify text in a way that can be recognised by a word processor and used when a word, phrase or paragraph is to be copied, moved or deleted as a block.

mass storage The storage of data on a number of magnetic disks. Also known as **backing storage**.

matrix The master in phototypesetting from which typed images are formed.

matrix printer A printer in which each character is made up of a series of dots produced by a print head pushing a pattern of wires against a ribbon and on to the paper; the head also moves across the paper. Dot matrix printers do not usually produce letter quality output. Also known as **dot matrix printer**.

MB Megabyte (one million bytes). Used to measure storage capacity of a computer.

measure   A printing term referring to the length of a line e.g. in pica spaces, in elite spaces.

measured block   A block of text of a fixed number of lines. Contrast with **variable block**.

mechanical memory   A term used to refer to backing storage and also known as auxiliary memory or **mass storage**.

media   Plural of medium.

medium   Any material used to store information e.g. magnetic disk, magnetic tape. The word is often used in the plural: media.

megabyte   1048576 bytes frequently referred to as one million bytes and used to measure storage capacity of a computer or central processing unit.

memo   A short and more common name for memorandum.

memorandum   Memoranda (plural) form a widely used communication channel in an organisation. Their purpose is to convey information, instructions or requirements, seek information, confirm information, make modifications, outline progress, seek assistance or co-operation, providing a written record of communication. Memos are initialled rather than signed.

memory   A device in the central processing unit of a computer which can store information for extraction by the computer when required. Memory is measured in bytes with each byte representing one character, letter, number, symbol, etc. The amount of memory is an indication of the computer's power; the larger the memory, the greater the power.

memory typewriter   An electronic typewriter which has a fixed memory. Some machines store a few characters for the typing of words or short phrases such as 'Yours faithfully', whilst others can store a number of characters sufficient to repeat whole paragraphs or standard phrases or sentences as and when required.

menu A list of possible options or facilities presented to the user from data or word processing software on a computer. Choice is normally displayed on the VDU of a terminal and selection is made via the keyboard.

merge The combining of information from two or more sources e.g. address lists or mailing lists with document files or form letters.

message A group of words, fixed or varied in length, transmitted between a terminal and a computer.

message switching In telecommunications, a technique which enables a computer to receive and store a message until the recipient is available, at which point the message is transmitted without the need for physical connection between outgoing and incoming lines.

message switching facility A device connected to an telephone extension which lights up if a connection has been attempted but not answered, indicating to the user that there is a message waiting.

messaging A form of electronic communication in which a message is sent directly to its destination e.g. telex.

Met Office Short for Meteorological Office.

Meteorological Office The office which predicts the weather and which gives weather reports in different parts of the country. A useful facility for a secretary whose boss is travelling to a meeting some distance away.

MICR Magnetic ink character recognition.

micro A microcomputer and a category for the smallest computers which use a microprocessor as its processing element.

microcomputer A category for the smallest computers which uses a microprocessor as its processing element, having sufficient peripherals and memory to link with the outside world and store information. The smallest forms of micro consist of a VDU with keyboard, screen display and microprocessor which acts as a central processing unit.

microelectronics   The use of integrated circuits in electronic devices.

microfiche   A form of microfilm where pages of text are photographically reduced and mounted onto a frame (as in a negative). Microfiche can be read a frame at a time using a microfiche reader.

microfiche directory   A list, usually alphabetical, listing all documents or information available on microfiche and kept in a relevant department. Major libraries are currently using microfiche listing of all their publications.

microfiche reader   An optical device which will illuminate frames of microfiche and provide an enlarged image which can be projected onto a screen to be read by the user.

microfilm   A type of microform in which pages of text are photographically reduced in sequence onto a roll of film. Microfilm is often used as a filing process which is developed to copy all kinds of material in reduced form for storing e.g. newspapers on microfilm.

microfilm reader   An optical device which will magnify each page of microfilm and present the image in an enlarged form on a screen which can then be read by the user.

microfilm reader/printer   A microfilm reader which can produce full size copies of the microfilm images when required.

micronet   A communication network for microcomputer users in the United Kingdom.

microprocessor   Sometimes a synonym for microcomputer but more correctly the central processor in which all elements of a control unit are contained on a single chip.

Midnight Line Service   A British Telecom service enabling an unlimited number of inland STD calls to be made between midnight and 6.00 am daily. Users pay a rental for each exchange line and a connection charge. The Midnight Line Service can be used in conjunction with the Datel services.

minicomputer A medium sized computer, smaller than mainframe but larger than micro with either general or specialised usage including process control, often used by a medium sized company to keep records, payroll, stock, etc.

minutes A written record of the business conducted at a meeting identified by the title which includes the name of the organisation, the type of meeting, venue and date. Paragraphs of minutes follow the order of the agenda and are numbered for easy reference. Minutes are a brief summary of major arguments of the meeting, followed by a recording of the decision made.

MIS Management information system.

mobile data system An information system which can be operated via a personal computer to transmit hard copy messages to vehicles, moving or stationary, manned or unmanned. It offers increased efficiency in the use of crowded airwaves of private mobile radio sector. The system is comprised of one base station connected to AM or FM radio base stations giving operators access to a number of mobile printer units installed in vehicles. Printed messages may therefore be passed between base and mobile, and the mobile may communicate with base by pressing a selection or pre-coded keys.

modem Modulator/demodulator. A device for converting a digital signal from a computer into an analogue signal which can then be transmitted along a standard telephone line. The received signal can be reconverted from analogue to digital by the same device at the receiving end.

monitor (1) Hardware or software used to monitor a computer system to detect deviations from pre-set conditions. (2) A synonym for an operating system. (3) A cathode ray tube used to monitor the quality of a television picture.

Mono Callmaker One of the types of Callmaker facilities offered by British Telecom for use over the telephone network. A telephone can be programmed to call one number of the operator's choice at the press of a button. The programmed number can easily be changed and the telephone can be used to call numbers other than the programmed number in the normal way.

monospacing   Letters typed all of the same set and width as on a standard typewriter. Compare with **proportional spacing**.

mouse   A device which can be rolled across the surface of a graphics table. When a button on the mouse is depressed, the computer will address the item in the mouse position. Commonly used with icons.

movement   The moving around of text within word processing where blocks of text are marked making them a marked or measured block and moved to other parts of a document or to another document.

MS DOS   A commercial name for a **disk operating system**.

multi-strike   An ink ribbon available for electronic typewriters or printers which is struck by the keys at different points vertically on the ribbon and which is often used to produce bold print.

multi-user   A computer system capable of handling the requirements of many users at the same time.

mute button   A button found on some telephones which when depressed allows the user to make privacy comments inaudible to the person on the other end of the line. During this time the call remains connected.

Nn

national calls Telephone calls made over the telephone network at a distance of more than 56 kilometres from the operating equipment and charged at a more expensive rate than local calls but less than international calls.

National Insurance A statutory deduction made from a salary or wage. At present there are six classes which specify different amounts of contribution dependent upon the personal circumstances of the individual, the amount of contribution of the employer and whether or not the individual is self-employed. National Insurance covers unemployment benefit, sickness benefit, payment for injury sustained at work, maternity allowance, widow's pension, retirement pension and death grant.

NCR No carbon required. Chemically impregnated paper which produces an image on second and subsequent sheets of paper upon impact.

net The amount of salary or wage earned after statutory and voluntary deductions have been made, sometimes referred to as 'take home pay' or 'take home figure'.

net profit The amount of money earned from the sale of goods or services after the deduction of costs of material, labour and all other overheads that may have been incurred in the production of those goods.

network A computer system where a number of components at a physical distance from each other can be inter-connected by telecommunications channels.

newspapers on microfilm A facility offered by many major libraries to hold past copies of newspapers on microfilm which is an efficient method of storing bulk items.

night busying A facility of the PABX switchboard which will operate on selected extensions only. After close of business, incoming calls may be automatically transferred to pre-determined extensions by setting engaged signals on those extensions not required.

night service A method of deferring calls from a main switchboard after close of business. There are three main types: (1) Unattended night service—bells are located around the company's premises. When a call is incoming, all bells ring and anyone who hears them may pick up the telephone, dial 8 and receive the call. (2) Exchange lines routed to specific extensions. Sometimes referred to as 'changed identity', night service numbers may be different from the daytime extension numbers. Senior management may be contacted by people who know their night service number. (3) Night service switchboard—calls are re-routed from the main switchboard to a smaller switchboard automatically. The smaller switchboards may be manned by a security officer and incoming calls are limited.

Nightstar A letter and parcel delivery service offered by the Post Office which guarantees to transport goods overnight for delivery the following morning.

no carbon required Chemically impregnated paper which produces an image on second and subsequent sheets on impact without the use of interleaved carbon paper. Also known as NCR paper.

non-impact printing Printers which do not require physical impact for printing characters on paper, e.g. ink jet printing and electrostatic printing. Contrast with **impact printing**.

number unobtainable tone A high-pitched continuous tone sounded when a telephone number which has been dialled is obsolete or out of order. It is common practice when the tone is heard for the user to ask the telephone operator to check the number, as it is possible that the number has been changed and the operator will have a note of the new one.

numeric keypad A keyboard using numbers only, like the keypad of a calculator.

numerical filing A popular filing classification system under which all files are numbered consecutively as they are raised and are stored in numerical order. Unlimited expansion is possible. A separate index usually has to be maintained on an alphabetical basis so that the number of any particular file may be found.

Oo

OCR   Optical character recognition. Characters printed on a document in a way that can be read both by an observer and by computer OCR readers.

off-line   A terminal or other computer component not connected to or controlled by a central processing unit. Contrast with **on-line**.

off-set litho   Off-set lithography.

off-set lithography   A method of printing by which many copies of an original document can be obtained from one plate. Image areas on the plate are coated with a water repellent ink whilst non-image areas are protected from the ink by a film of water. Working on the theory that oil and water do not mix, the printer's ink from the roller will stick only to the image.

on-line   A terminal or other component directly connected to the central processing unit in a computer system and which will interact directly with the central processor. Contrast with **off-line**.

open punctuation   The use of punctuation marks in text only where they are absolutely necessary, e.g. the use of full stops at the end of sentences and the use of commas to separate the difference in meaning of phrases. The rest of the text uses no punctuation, e.g. an address would show no full stops or commas.

operating software   Software used to run the operating system of a computer. Compare with **applications software**.

operating system   A collection of programs contained in a computer used to control the sequencing of processing of other programs (like applications programs) from the operation of various input and output devices.

operator service   A switchboard operated by British Telecom and used over the telephone network which is manned 24 hours a day. The facility is available to subscribers having difficulty obtaining a call, or requiring other services offered by Telecom, e.g. ADC, alarm call.

optical character reader   A machine which reads printed letters, numbers or symbols and compares them with those stored in its memory generating that letter, number or symbol in a computer readable form. Sometimes known as OCR.

optical character recognition   A technique in which information in the form of characters, numbers or symbols is read by an optical scanning device, or optical character reader, which converts the information into computer readable form. Also known as **OCR**.

optical fibre   A thin flexible fibre of pure glass able to carry 1000 times the information possible with copper wire. Lasers and light emitting diodes are two main light sources used with optical fibres. Telecommunications can occur by passing light down bundles of continuous glass fibres. Also known as **fibre optics**.

optical mark recognition   Marks made using a pencil, ballpoint pen or typewriter in pre-defined areas of a document, which can be read by a machine and the information converted into computer readable form. Sometimes referred to as OMR.

Oracle®   Optical reception of announcements by coded line electronics. The teletext system of the British Independent Television Authority in the United Kingdom.

order The first of a series of documents produced in a sales transaction bearing a reference number, quantities, description and quoted prices of goods that are required to be purchased by one company from another. A signed order form is a commitment to purchase.

output Information transmitted by a computer or its storage devices to a screen or printer. It may be in the form of print on paper, punched cards or paper tape.

output device A device capable of receiving information from a central processor or peripheral unit which translates computer information into another medium e.g. a VDU, printer.

overhead projector A visual method of presenting data by the use of a transparency which has been prepared either by writing, drawing or typing directly onto acetate sheets called overhead projector transparencies, or by photocopying onto transparencies from documents or diagrams using a thermal copier. The transparency is placed onto an overhead projector and the image is magnified and displayed above the projector so that it can be seen by a group of people.

overwriting The writing of data into a computer's memory where data previously held in a location is replaced with the new data. Compare with **insert**.

overwrite mode When a computer keyboard is in overwrite mode, any data written to the screen and then into the memory replaces the data previously written to that location. Compare with **insert mode**.

Pp

PABX Private automatic branch exchange. A telephone system which allows outgoing calls to be dialled direct from an extension without the assistance of the switchboard operator. It has a facility for the switchboard operator to inform callers that another call is waiting to be connected if the extension is engaged by the emission of a high pitched bleep. Compare with **PBX**.

package A computer program or collection of programs written to cover the requirements of a number of users. A package applies to an application, e.g. stock control, and is versatile enough to cater for a large number of different requirements.

packet switchstream services The name given to the service of packet switching and a method of routing data or messages from a transmitter to a receiver.

packet switched/switching A method of routing data or messages from a transmitter to a receiver which splits a message up into small packets. This splitting may be carried out at the transmitting terminal or at an exchange, each packet containing the address of the message's destination. At the reception point, packets have to be sorted and re-assembled. There are two main techniques of packet switching: (1) Autonomous mode where each packet is individually sent within the network according to the address attached to it. (2) Virtual link mode where a pre-established route is followed within the network for each packet.

packet tying machine A machine usually found in the mail room of large distribution companies which ties up parcels so that they are secure for distribution. A labour saving device which can improve the speed and efficiency of the department.

page breaks   In word processing, an internal command which informs the printer to start a new page. This is handled automatically on some systems according to the pre-determined length of page.

page control   A feature of word processors which allows the operator to address the length of the typing page to suit the display of text or omit pages of typed text which will still be numbered chronologically within the document for the later insertion of diagrams or drawings.

page feed   A facility of most printers to roll up the paper one page at a time through the printing mechanism. This is usually possible via the printer direct from a key panel positioned on the printer itself, or via the software in use at the time.

page-based system   A feature of some word processing programs where each file is produced in pages making up a whole document. The hard copy output is the same as it appears on the screen of a VDU. It is common in this type of program to find a length of document status line indicating the number of full pages used and the number of lines used on incomplete pages. Compare with **document based system**.

pagination   (1) The numbering of pages in a document.   (2) A word processing function used to create and number pages. Pagination on screen can be varied, sometimes indicated by a marker appearing on the screen between two lines of text.

paging device   (1) A variation of a public address or loudspeaker system used to call the attention of an individual to receive a message. Paging device systems are often used in airport lounges, hotels and other large organisations.   (2) A small pocket radio receiver activated from a central control board. The recipient hears a signal which informs him/her that he/she is being 'paged' and that he/she needs to contact the central control board operator.

paper tape   See **perforated tape**.

parallel bit transmission   A data transmission system where the bits representing the characters are transmitted simultaneously.

parallel interface   An interface which permits parallel bit transmission. Compare with **serial interface**.

parking calls   A facility available to the operator of a telephone switchboard connected to the telephone network, where the extension required by an incoming call is engaged. The incoming call may be 'parked' in a store while the operator fulfils other duties but will be connected upon the busy extension becoming free.

PASCAL   Program Appliqué à la Selection et la Compilation Automatique de la Litterature. A large multidisciplinary database compiled by the French Centre Nationale de la Recherche Scientifique. Sometimes referred to as a high level language used for general programming work.

password   A set of characters which a user inputs to a computer, which the computer will use to identify the user, and by the correct use of which entry to the computer system may be gained. Passwords are used to protect computer systems against unauthorised access and are made up of a combination of letters, numbers or symbols.

pay advice   A piece of paper accompanying cash or cheque received by way of wage or salary. Often a salary slip without cash or cheque is an indication of a pay advice. It gives details of gross pay earned that week or month and to date in the current tax year, the amount of statutory deductions made for income tax and national insurance, superannuation deductions, voluntary deductions, the individual's payroll number, bonus, overtime and finally the net amount of pay.

payfone   Public telephones connected to the telephone network from which calls may be made locally, nationally or internationally and which operate in the same way and offer the same facilities as a private telephone. The caller pays for the call before it is made by inserting coins into the machine.

pay tone   A series of high pitched bleeps emitted when a caller dials a telephone number on a payfone and when the recipient of the call lifts the receiver. When the pay tone is heard, the money for the call should be inserted into the telephone box. The pay tone is presently being phased out by British Telecom who are producing in its place a telephone into which money is inserted before the number is dialled and which is returned if the call is not connected.

PAYE   Pay as you earn. Employees of a company are liable to pay income tax on income earned. Tax is collected by employers by a system known as PAYE and paid on behalf of employees to the Inland Revenue. Individual employees are given a tax code on the basis of details furnished by them to the Inland Revenue who will offset allowances against income tax to be paid.

payroll   A complete list of employees' names against which all details of pay and deductions for the week including employer's contributions are entered. The pay advice sheet which the employee receives is an identical copy of his or her entry on a payroll.

PBX   Private branch exchange. An internal telephone system not connected to the public telephone network. Used for inter-department communication a PBX system leaves outside lines free for incoming calls. Compare with **PABX**.

PC   Personal computer. A microcomputer suitable for use in the home.

peak rate call   A call made via the telephone network at the time when it is the most expensive i.e. 9.00 am to 1.00 pm Monday to Friday.

pending file   Often referred to as document retention i.e. how long papers should be kept by an organisation. There are four definitions: (1) Permanent retention—documents such as deeds, share certificates, insurance policies.

(2) Semi-permanent retention (usually up to six years)—invoices, receipts, etc. (3) Retention for twelve months—current correspondence, quotations, etc. which are usually destroyed after two or three years. (4) Temporary retention—filing which may only be kept a few weeks or months, e.g. a telephone enquiry about a product which does not materialise into an order.

perforated tape A computer input/output medium in the form of a strip of paper in which data is represented by small holes punched in rows across the tape. Also known as **paper tape**.

perforation A way of making a continuous roll of stationery separable by punching holes horizontally across at standardised intervals (often A4 size) in order that one sheet of paper may easily be torn from another.

peripheral Any unit of a computer e.g. disk drive, joystick, light pen, card reader, magnetic tape unit, printer, which connect in different ways to the central processor and memory and which form input and output devices.

peripheral interchange program A method of moving data between two peripheral units in the form of a computer program. Also known as **PIP**.

person-to-person call A call made via the operator on the telephone network for which the charge becomes payable only when the recipient of the call is brought to the telephone. Also known as **personal call**.

personal call A facility available through the operator of the telephone network. If a receptionist is having difficulty contacting a person, perhaps at a conference or in an hotel, he/she may book a personal call with the operator. A fee is payable for this service, although the charge for the call does not commence until the person required is brought to the telephone. Only one fee is payable for the call, despite the number of attempts made to contact the person within 24 hours of the call being placed.

personal computer   Basically a microcomputer suggesting that the computer is suitable for use in the home, although technically many personal computers are used in business environments. Also known as **PC**.

photocopier   A machine which will reproduce an exact copy of an original document through the action of heat, electrostatic charge or light. Accurate copies are produced without the need for a skilled operator. Drawings, graphs and even photographs in some cases can be copied direct from an original document.

phototypesetting   The production of type images on a photographic medium by optical means and often a computer connected to a device which enables publication with high quality print.

pica   In typography, a measurement of length, referring to ten typewritten characters to the horizontal inch.

PIP   Peripheral interchange program. A method of moving data between two peripheral units, including disk to disk by means of a computer program.

pitch   The number of characters that will fit into one inch of a line of text, typically 10, 12 or 15 when the typed text is monospaced.

plain paper copier   A photocopier which can produce an image from the original on ordinary paper where the drum in the unit receives a static charge. The image is formed on the drum and transferred to the paper by an electrostatic process.

plan filing   Drawings and plans are usually stored flat in drawers or upright in cabinets containing compartments with dividers enabling storage without bending. Indexing is done by means of indexing strips.

PL/1   Programming language/1. A high level computer programming language with a wide range of scientific and business applications.

plotter   A computer controlled output device which will print output from graphics software.

PMBX   Private manual branch exchange. A telephone system where all incoming and outgoing telephone calls are routed through the switchboard operator, allowing the operator the facility to monitor all outgoing calls. Compare with **PABX, PBX**.

point of sale terminal   Electronic terminals used at retail outlets (often supermarket check-outs) which record a financial transaction as it happens.

portfolio   A computer program which assists companies who have invested in the stocks and shares of other companies, producing reports, giving current value of investment and return on investment.

POS   Point of sale terminal.

Post Office Guide   A book published annually by Her Majesty's Stationery Office giving complete information on all departments of the Post Office including inland and overseas services and charges, postal rates and conditions, telecommunications, savings schemes and all related services. Supplements are issued throughout the year.

post rate scales   A booklet published by Her Majesty's Stationery Office available at most main Post Offices which lists the weights and costs of letters and parcels inland and overseas, first and second class post.

postage stamp machine   A machine still found in some mail rooms, although to a large extent these have been replaced with franking machines. A roll of stamps is locked into the machine which records the postage as stamps are used. Some machines have several rolls of stamps of different values.

Postal Address and Index to Postcode Directory   A directory containing the correct postal addresses including postcodes in the United Kingdom and Irish Republic.

postal charges Charges for the mailing of letters and parcels, first and second class post, the rates for which can be found in the HMSO publication Post Office Guide.

poste restante Letters or parcels to be called for may be addressed to any Post Office with the words 'to be called for' or 'poste restante' appearing in the address line. Collectors must produce proof of identity. The service is intended for travellers and may not be used in the same location for more than three months.

Prestel® A public viewdata (interactive videotex) system implemented by British Telecom using the public telephone system. Prestel transmits text, pictures and diagrams and other images on a television screen, providing a public information service which can be used in home and business. It is a flexible form of a computer based information retrieval system.

printer An output device from a computer which produces hard copy (text on paper) concerned with speed, quality and price.

printing head The part of the printer that actually does the printing of characters, numbers and symbols onto the paper. Types of printing head can be golfball (now becoming obsolete), daisy wheel or dot matrix.

print out The reproduction of text (printed paper output) on paper which a computer produces via a printer. In data processing the term can often refer to a wide ruled paper tractor fed through the printer and printed at very high speed.

print pause A command facility of most computer programs which stops the printer for paper change, ribbon change, paper jam, etc. automatically. On some printers print can be paused at any point and re-started on the user's command.

print wheel A wheel which can be easily changed when necessary made up of stalks onto the ends of which characters, numbers and symbols are attached which is used to print characters in some types of printer e.g. daisy wheel printer.

private bag A lockable bag offering the facility for the posting and receipt of correspondence. The bag is taken to and from the Post Office by the user or by the postman (for an additional fee). The bag and key are supplied by the user.

private box A box for incoming mail which can be rented from the Post Office for the reception and delivery of postal packets as an alternative to normal delivery thus making it possible to obtain delivery of the packets before the normal delivery service. The service is often quoted as a reply service in advertisements under a box number reference.

processor The central processing unit comprises the processor and a certain amount of immediate storage (memory). The processor is the central point at which various devices are connected, usually based on a microprocessor together with links to each of the various peripheral units. Synonymous with central processor.

profit and loss A bookkeeping term referring to an account compiled at the end of a financial year showing the year's revenue and expense items and indicating gross and net profit or loss. A profit and loss computer program takes into account all stock, stock sold, returns, stock in manufacture, expenses, salaries, direct expenditure, which can ease the production of a profit and loss account.

program A set of instructions which a computer carries out in sequence enabling the computer to operate and carry out specific tasks.

program generator The term usually refers to report program generator which is a general purpose program enabling computer output to be formatted in a report form specified by the user's requirements.

programmable Capable of storing and executing an ordered list of instructions.

programmable read only memory With the use of special equipment, read only memory which can be programmed. Also known as **PROM**.

programming language The language in which coded instructions are written for a computer. Also known as **high level language** or **low level language**.

Programming Language/1 A high level computer programming language. Attempts have been made to produce a single and uniform programming language, an example of which is PL/1, avoiding the need for a multitude of programming languages. Also known as **PL/1**.

PROM Programmable read only memory. A chip which can be programmed by the user. Once programmed its contents are non-volatile.

prompt A computer initiated message to the operator used to indicate that particular information is required before the program can proceed any further.

proportional spacing The spacing of typewritten characters in proportion to their size. Standard typewriters produce letters of uniform width, e.g. a capital L gets the same space as a lower case l, irrespective of their size. Typewriters which offer a facility for proportional spacing allow less space to a small l, than the space they allow to a capital L.

protocol A set of standards which govern a format of communications to be exchanged between two devices in a communications system.

PSS Packet switching service. A method of routing data or messages from a transmitter to a receiver which splits the message into small packets.

PSTN Public switched telephone network. In telecommunications the means of inter-connecting users via telephone exchanges for the distribution of computer data. PSTN is a wide area network.

public address system Operating through loudspeakers connected to a microphone, a public address system can be used for making public announcements. It is often an integral part of a PABX telephone exchange and is invaluable in cases of emergencies, e.g. fire in the building.

public data network A database system allowing members of the public to access information. A charge is made for this service and subscribers may require special equipment such as a modem and a terminal. An example of a public data network is Prestel.

public switched telephone network In telecommunications, a wide area network in use by British Telecom inter-connecting users. Switching is carried out by telephone exchanges but other types of switching are available for special purposes, circuit switching, message switching, packet switching.

punched card A card of standard size used to input data and instructions to a computer. Holes are punched into the card into a pattern determined by the code used by the card punch. Holes can be read by a computer and then coded as characters or numbers. There are two main types: the 80 column and the 96 column, holding up to 80 and 96 digits, alphabetic letters or symbols respectively.

punched card machine A device allowing the reading of information which has been punched on cards and the conversion of this information into electronic messages which can be read by a computer.

punched index An indexing system for use with punched cards.

punched tape A method of storing information for use on computers working in a similar way to punched card except that tape is in strips or rolls depending upon the amount of information stored.

Qq

queue The processing of jobs or items e.g. data awaiting action, execution or transmission. If terminals in a multi-user system send a file for printing simultaneously, the files will be queued and printed in rotation.

qwerty keyboard A keyboard which has the keys laid out as that used on standard typewriters. The word derives from the letters at the top left hand side of the keyboard.

Rr

RAC Handbook A handbook produced by the Royal Automobile Club which gives details of the services of the organisation, as well as information about hotels, maps and garages. See also **AA Handbook**.

radiopaging Employees who are regularly out of the office may need to be contacted and can be issued with a pocket sized personal radio receiver, sometimes referred to as a 'bleeper' system, as the receiver bleeps sending out a high pitched signal when activiated from a central control point usually a switchboard. When the signal is received, the recipient reports to the nearest telephone and calls the control unit.

radiophone Generally a one- or two-way radio. In a one-way system, a spoken message can be transmitted directly to the receiver, used e.g. from aircraft with communication from air to ground only. In a two-way radio system known also as a 'walkie-talkie' messages can be received and transmitted and is used e.g. in ships for ship to shore communication and vice versa. For a two-way radio system a special Post Office licence is required together with the allocation of a wavelength for the operation.

Rail Express Europe An expedient parcel and letter delivery facility offered by the Post Office where mail is sent by high speed train to its destination.

railway letters By agreement with the Post Office certain railway stations are able to accept first class letters for transmission on railway lines to the destination station. Letters may be collected from the destination station or transferred to the local post sorting office.

RAM Random access memory.

random access Direct access to a record's store in any location on a storage medium where usually access time to any location is the same. Contrasts with **sequential access**. Also known as **random access storage**.

random access memory Memory into which information can be written and from which it may read in a random access fashion. The size of a computer's random access memory is a measure of the computer's power. Also known as **RAM**.

reformat A feature of most word processors, whereby after the insertion, modification or deletion of text in a file, the format of the file can automatically be readjusted to give a good finished copy within the pre-set margins or line length.

repagination Automatic alteration of page numbering and size which is a feature of most word processors and which is normally used after the editing of text, particularly in document-based systems.

read The copying of information from a storage medium, or the electronic retrieval of information.

read only A term used in reference to memory and magnetic disks. If the disk has been write protected, the contents of the disk can be read but nothing can be written to it. This facility provides a safeguard against the accidental erasure of data, information and programs stored on a disk.

read only memory A store of memory from which information can only be read or copied. Read only memory is usually a permanent store holding software which is permanently or firmly in place. Also known as **ROM** and sometimes referred to as **firmware**.

read/write head An electro-magnetic device which is used to read information from or write information to a magnetic storage device.

read/write memory   Information in a computer memory which can be accessed and read or changed (written to). Compare with **read only memory**.

real time   A computer system is said to be operating in real time if the system operates synchronously, responding to a request from a terminal and the processing of information which is fed in takes place straightaway. An example of a real time system is a system used for airline reservations.

ream   A quantity of paper, namely 500 sheets.

record   A group of related fields forming the basic elements of a file and a complete piece of information e.g. name and address.

record length   Records can be of variable length according to the amount of data input into each field. Fields are usually of fixed length allowing for a maximum number of characters to be entered, although it may be appropriate that some fields may be made up of spaces, thus making the overall length of a record of a variable nature.

recorded delivery   A Post Office service and an alternative to registered post. Less expensive than registered post, proof of delivery of a letter or parcel can be obtained. A compensation of fee (less than that for registered post) is payable in the event of loss.

recorded message   Recorded messages are used with telephone answering machines. After the close of business, a caller may ring an organisation and hear a recorded message if the organisation uses a telephone answering machine. The recorded message is used to give the caller information and may be changed to suit the requirements or the activities of the business.

Red Star   A national delivery service where parcels are taken to the nearest railway station and left at a destination station closest to the address on the parcel from where they can be collected by the addressee or a representative of the addressee company.

Red Star Europe A facility similar to Red Star but operating into Europe.

Red Star Flyover A facility similar to Red Star but one which uses aircraft instead of trains with delivery to the nearest airport and collection from the nearest destination airport to the address on the parcel.

Red Star One Stop London A service similar to Red Star but direct to London and offering a speedier and more efficient delivery on a one-stop-only basis.

re-direction A facility offered by the Post Office for which a fee is payable for a private individual or company which has moved address. All mail for a specified period of time will be intercepted at the sorting office and automatically re-routed to the new address.

reference An alphabetical, numerical or alphanumeric string appearing at the top of a letter, memo, invoice, order, etc. which usually refers to a file number or filing sequence within the organisation.

register A memory which acts temporarily to collect data before it is sent to a peripheral device. Also known as **buffer memory**.

registered post A service offered by the Post Office for the transmission of money through the post. A registered envelope can be purchased from the Post Office or one similar to it can be used. There is a fee payable for this service and some compensation is available in the event of loss.

reminder system A method of filing sometimes referred to as a tickler file. Reminder systems are used when a topic cannot be instantly dealt with. Receipt of the incoming enquiry is acknowledged and the original letter, together with the copy reply is filed in the reminder system to be dealt with at a later date. A typical example of a reminder filing system would be a file with numerical divisions for days of the month (1–31). It is therefore important that the filing system is checked daily.

remote access   The use of a computer from a terminal situated somewhere other than in the computer room. The terminal may be connected to the computer by cables or broadcast transmission.

remote control   Control of a device or activity from a distant location using radio, electrical or ultrasonic signals.

remote dictation system   A dictation system often used by newspapers for reporters to dictate their copy to a machine rather than to a shorthand writer. Users can dictate their message or reports onto a dictation machine or telephone recording machine after making an initial telephone call to a receiving telephone.

remote station   A terminal in communication with a processor situated somewhere other than with the processor.

renaming   A facility of most computers to change the name given to one file to something different. This makes for a very flexible filing system.

repeat function   A facility of most computer keyboards and electronic typewriters to repeat the last key typed and useful in the drawing of straight lines or lines of dots as in the preparation of a questionnaire and for automatic scrolling from the top to the bottom of a document when proof reading.

replicate   A facility available in spreadsheet programs that when a formula for calculations has been set up, the formula can be copied to other cells made up of a specified row and column automatically without the need for the formula to be redefined.

report program   A program which has been designed to print out the analysis of a data file.

report program generator   A general purpose program which can be used for producing a variety of output reports specific to the user's requirements. Report program generator has now been developed into a programming language.

resolution The sharpness of detail distinguishable in an image e.g. a high resolution screen refers to a visual display unit which shows fineness of detail in an image.

response time The time it takes for a computer to reply to a command given to it by a user e.g. the time it takes between the operator pressing a key on the keyboard and the displaying of the character on the screen of the VDU.

retrieve The way in which a computer searches for particular files or parts of files in response to a request from a user and loads those files to the cursor or screen. An information retrieval system provides information to users in response to requests made of it.

return A key on a computer keyboard and electronic and electric typewriters which when depressed automatically returns the cursor or carriage to the start of the next line.

reverse printer A printer capable of printing right to left, and left to right. Also known as a **bi-directional printer**.

ribbon A reel of durable inked material which will spool right to left and vice versa over the printing point of a typewriter or printer. Ribbons are generally housed in a compact unit for ease of removal and replacement.

ringing tone A continual 'burr burr' sound made when a telephone number has been dialled, connected through the telephone exchange and is ringing at the destination point.

road conditions A telephone service offered by British Telecom particularly useful to executives when travelling to distant locations. A series of numbers are specified for different regions. The caller selects and dials the required number for a report of the weather and road conditions for that area.

rolling and wrapping machine A machine found in the mail room of large distribution organisations designed to perform the purely mechanical function of preparing parcels for posting i.e. placing goods into special envelopes or boxes, sealing the flaps and labelling at high speed.

ROM   Read only memory. A permanent store of memory which can be read but cannot normally be changed.

rotary index   An index system where the cards are stored in a metal cabinet with a central spine. When the spine is rotated by a wheel, the user can read the cards making alteration to them without removing them by inserting a small metal plate behind the selected card.

row   A line of a matrix appearing horizontally across the screen from left to right numbered chronologically from the top of the screen (as 1, 2, 3 downwards etc.).

Royal Mail Special Delivery   A Post Office facility which makes arrangements for a letter to be specially delivered from the Post Office in the area of the addressee before the normal delivery service. Also known as **express delivery**.

rubber stamp   A paid produced by stationery companies bearing some kind of information which can be used on many documents. Information held on the stamps suits the user's needs. The process works with the use of an inked pad onto which the rubber stamp is placed. The stamp is then placed on the document where an inked impression will be made.

ruler line   In word processing a line across the top or bottom of a visual display unit screen which indicates the margin positions and the tabulation which has been set.

run   The execution of a computer program, suite of programs or routine.

Ss

salary A fixed annual sum of money made in return for employment paid by equal monthly instalments. Method of payment is normally into a bank, Post Office or building society account.

salutation The greeting phrase of a letter which may be personal when the addressee is known to the writer (Dear Mr Smith, Dear Mary) or impersonal when the address is not known (Dear Sir, Dear Madam).

save A computing term used to refer to the storing of data on storage media e.g. on magnetic disks. In order to ensure that work is not accidentally abandoned without being saved, most computer systems have a safeguard prompt.

scales In business, the term generally refers to salary scales which is the payment of employees according to grades. This has a number of advantages; employees are aware that they are being paid the correct rate for the job as scales are defined for different categories of work; rates of pay for higher grades are known and employees can assess their promotion prospects; secrecy with regard to pay and arbitrary increases are removed.

scan The examination of material e.g. a word processing document, a page of a document or the conversion of data into machine readable form.

scratch file The termination of a file after work has been done on it. Contrasts with a permanent file stored in the memory for later use.

screen The surface of a cathode ray terminal where data can be displayed. Often referred to as a **visual display unit**.

scroll   The movement of text up and down or across a visual display unit so that the user can view the whole of a document or, on systems that display only half pages, the whole of a page.

search   An examination of information in a computer file to find the occurrence of a character, word or phrase. A search of a document is normally carried out from the place where the cursor is positioned to the end of a document.

search and replace   A word processing facility in which every occurrence of a specified character, word or phrase is replaced with a pre-defined character, word or phrase. Also known as **global exchange** or **global search and replace**.

second class post   The Post Office offers two postal delivery services for letters in the UK; first and second class. Second class is less expensive but letters take a few days to be delivered after posting. An adequate system for non-urgent literature or correspondence.

sector   An addressable part of a magnetic disk constituting the smallest unit of memory.

selectapost   A facility offered from local post sorting offices where an addressee's mail is sorted into sections before it is delivered. Indication of the divisions must appear as part of the address. Arrangements for this facility are made with the post sorting office for a minimum of one year.

selective sort   A computer routine which takes items from a list one at a time, depositing those items into a second list until the whole of the first list has been scanned. Compare with **bubble sort**.

semi-blocked letters   A type of display for business letters where all lines except the first line of a paragraph, the heading and the complimentary close start against the left hand margin. Paragraphs are normally indented, headings can be centred and the complimentary close starts at the centre of the page.

sequential access The storage and retrieval of records and information which has been recorded in sequence e.g. on magnetic tape. Any information which needs to be accessed will be searched for in an order of start to finish, so that all text is passed over until the required text is encountered. Compare with **random access**.

sequential storage The storage of records in an order where the next available space after the storage of the previous record is used.

serial The travelling of electrical patterns of bits down a wire to a computer, one after the other often referred to as serial bit stream.

serial access The storage and retrieval of data in a sequential fashion where each record is accessed by the scanning of start to finish until the required location is encountered as on magnetic tape. Compare with **random access**. Same as **sequential access**.

serial bit transmission Slower than parallel bit transmission, a data transmission system where the bits that represent characters are transmitted one after another.

serial interface An interface in which access time involves a waiting time where serial bit transmission is used. Compare with **parallel interface**.

serial storage Storage on a magnetic device in which words appear in sequence often inferring that access time will include a waiting time.

shared facility A computer system in which several pieces of equipment use the same facility, e.g. a disk drive, a printer. Also known as **shared resource**.

shared logic A computer system consisting of work stations made up of keyboards and VDUs which are connected to a central processing unit, usually with a hard disk. The terminals operate under central control.

shared resource Several pieces of computer equipment which make use of the same facility e.g. storage, printer, disk drive. While such systems make most efficient use of the shared resource, careful planning needs to be ensured for efficient operation. Also known as **shared facility**.

shift A key on a typewriter or computer keyboard which when depressed and held down converts the small alpha characters into upper case and the numerical characters into symbols as marked above the numbers on the keyboard display.

signatory The name given to the person who signs his or her name in an official capacity e.g. a company cheque, business letters, etc.

silicon chip A wafer of silicon onto which an integrated electronic circuit is stamped.

simulation The use of a computer program to model the behaviour of a system or process.

single drum duplicator A duplicating machine consisting of a drum made of perforated metal covered with fabric, containing ink squeezed into it from a tube through the filler hole. As the drum rotates, ink is spread evenly through the fabric, transferring the image from the stencil onto paper. Compare with **twin drum duplicator**.

single element printer A fixed head printer fitted with a daisy wheel which revolves as the character to be printed is looked for. The daisy wheel head is interchangeable. Many single element printers are dual pitch (10 or 12 pitch) and some offer 15 pitch.

single line display A feature of memory typewriters and electronic typewriters where all typing is shown electronically on a small screen before the line is typed. Any errors can be corrected on the display before the line is printed.

single sheet feed The action of passing one sheet of paper through a printer. A piece of paper is inserted into the printer, the top of which is positioned near the print head.

When the printer has been turned on or the file sent for printing from the terminal, the first page of the document is printed. The printer will then pause for the insertion of a new sheet of paper.

soft copy   Computer output on a medium which cannot be read by an observer e.g. floppy disk or computer output as displayed on the screen of a visual display unit.

soft sectoring   By the use of recorded information, the marking of boundaries on magnetic disk. Contrast with **hard sectoring**.

software   A generic term for programs, operating systems, packages and compilers which are used to direct the operations of a computer or other hardware and which can be run on computer hardware, consisting of patterns of binary information. Software can be permanently or temporarily coded into a silicon chip or recorded on paper tape, magnetic disk or magnetic tape. Compare with **hardware**.

software house   A commercial organisation specialising in the design, preparation and writing of programs of software for clients.

sort   The arrangement of items of information into a meaningful order, often into alphabetical, numerical or chronological order.

space bar   A long bar at the base of the alpha keys on a typewriter or computer keyboard used for inserting spaces between characters or words.

speaking clock   A 24-hour facility offered by British Telecom via the public telephone network. By dialling a specified number the caller will be given the correct time accurate to one twentieth of a second.

speech generation   The production of human speech by a computer using a limited vocabulary where often the computer can read back the information given to it.

speech recognition The identification of human speech by a computer program which compares the sound of the words with words stored in its memory. If a match is found in the computer memory, the word is displayed or printed, or the instruction conveyed by the word is executed. Also known as **voice recognition**.

speech synthesis The production of speech using electronic means. At present devices for synthesising recognisable speech are toys and translation routines. Also known as **voice synthesis**.

spelling check A program available on most word processors which runs parallel to the word processing program itself. The program uses a standard or specialised dictionary which can be added to by the user. When the program is run, the text is checked for spelling errors offering the user the opportunity to make corrections.

spirit duplicator A machine used to produce multiple copy documents by the preparation of a master. The master is prepared by typing or writing on master paper against which a sheet of hecto carbon is placed enabling a reversed image to be obtained on the back of the master paper. The master is then fixed to the drum of the duplicator and as the drum is rotated, sheets of non-absorbent duplicating paper are fed through, damped with a fluid which activates a dye on the master, transferring the image the correct way round onto the duplicating paper.

split screen The displaying of more than one image on the screen of a VDU, e.g. a page of text may be shown in one section of the screen, whilst a page of a spreadsheet may be shown in a different area of the same screen at the same time. Areas of the screen are referred to as 'windows'.

split screen program A computer program which offers the facility to display more than one image on a screen at any one time allowing the examination of more than one document.

spreadsheet An application program which provides a matrix into which data can be entered and manipulated and intended for use in forecasting and financial planning.

sprocket-fed A method for advancing paper through a printer. The paper is edged with punched holes which engage onto spiked wheels as they rotate on a feeding mechanism.

stand-alone A piece of equipment which can operate independently of any other equipment e.g. a work station which can operate on its own without being connected with a central processing unit is a stand-alone system. Often a category for word processors which are self contained and require no additional equipment.

standard correction marks When text is proof read and corrections or changes made to it, each correction instruction can be indicated by a mark in the text with a corresponding mark in the margin to signify or explain the meaning of the mark. A classified list of the standard correction marks used for copy preparation and proof correction is issued by the British Standards Institution.

standard paragraphs In computing, specifically word processing, text that is frequently used, stored and available for insertion into assembled documents. A long document such as a lease could have many standard paragraphs.

standard rate calls Charges made for telephone calls that are made between 8 am and 9 am and after 1 pm and before 6 pm Monday to Friday inclusively.

standard text A facility of most word processors which enables the operator to store and recall rapidly and easily words and phrases and often paragraphs that are used frequently e.g. 'Yours sincerely', a company VAT registration number, etc.

status information Information communicated by the computer to the user to indicate the condition of a peripheral unit e.g. printer malfunction, or to indicate that the system is ready for the next input e.g. 'ready'.

status line Information displayed on the screen of a VDU indicating to the user factors relating to layout e.g. spacing, progress of work and the line currently in use.

statutory deduction Deductions made from a salary or wage for PAYE or National Insurance. Accumulated statutory deductions are passed by the employer to the appropriate government departments.

STD Subscriber trunk dialling. Direct dialling to a distant location by the use of a telephone code.

STD booklet A booklet issued by British Telecom to subscribers listing all national subscriber trunk dialling codes. It is becoming current practice to incorporate the dialling codes in the front of the White pages directory rather than publish a separate booklet.

stencil A sheet of paper coated with thin plastic which has a backing sheet attached to it. Stencils are 'cut' by the use of a typewriter without a ribbon (either the ribbon is removed or disengaged). As keys are struck, the surface of the stencil is broken. Stencils are used on stencil or ink duplicators. It is possible that after use, a stencil can be cleaned and stored for re-use.

stock The amount of physical goods that a company holds at any one time. As future profits depend on the sale of this stock, it is important that the stock is stored in adequate conditions to suit the goods and that access to stock is kept under control.

stock control The checks that are made upon the goods that a company holds at any one time. It is common practice in industry that regular checks of stock levels are made.

storage Another word for memory in a computer system, or the medium on which information can be stored.

stored data Data that has been saved or stored in a computer's memory or on backing storage e.g. magnetic disk and which can be retrieved when required.

strikeover A facility of most word processors to type one character over another character, so that both characters (letters, numbers, symbols or a combination of these) appear in one type space e.g. if a keyboard does not offer a dollar sign key, this can be made up by typing a letter s and overtyping with a | with the end result of $.

string A group of items which are arranged in sequence according to a set of pre-defined rules, e.g. a set of consecutive characters in a computer memory.

string search A facility of most word processors sometimes referred to as the find facility; when a string of characters is typed to the search, the file will be searched for where that string appears. Also known as **search facility**.

strip index A filing system based on sheets of cardboard strips onto which filenames can be typed or written. The strips are then placed onto metal plates capable of holding up to 70 strips. The plates are then housed in rotating desk stands or wall racks enabling the user to rotate the plates to search for the required file reference. This system of filing is often used as an index system where a filename can be incorporated onto one strip.

subject heading A line or two of type appearing at the top of a memo, business letter or report giving an indication as to the content of the document.

subscriber trunk dialling Direct dialling to a distance location by a telephone subscriber with the use of pre-defined numeric codes. Also known as **STD**.

subscript A character which lies below the normal line of type e.g. H_2O, CO_2.

subscription The closing phrase of a letter before the signature. If the salutation is impersonal, the subscription should read Yours faithfully or Yours truly. If the salutation is personal, the subscription should read as Yours sincerely. Also known as **complimentary close**.

superscript　A character that lies above the normal typed line e.g. $45°$, 3^2.

surface mail　A Post Office facility which carries letters and parcels overseas and overland to the destination address. Although the service takes longer than airmail, it is less expensive.

suspension file　A method of filing which uses cabinets with each file having the long opening edge strengthened by a metal bar. Hooks on the ends of the metal bar enable the files to be fitted into drawers so that the folders are suspended. Folders are then labelled across the top of the metal strip for easy identification.

switchboard　An external telephone installation which is connected to the telephone exchange. It is possible for a switchboard to have more than one exchange line and a multitude of internal extensions. There are three main types of switchboard; *strouger* using electrical and mechanical moving parts; *crossbar* using electronic and moving parts; and *electronic* which has no moving parts. Most PABX switchboards are examples of electronic switchboards.

synchronous transmission　The constant transmission of bits or characters. When applied to modems, a synchronous modem uses strictly timed data transfer for high speed transmission. Compare with **asynchronous transmission**.

system　An organised set of computer components which interact to allow the processing of data.

systems analyst　A person trained in the investigation, analysis and design of computer systems (often for business applications) who can provide solutions to the most effective way of processing data.

systems analysis　The task of analysing computer systems and determining how a computer system can be made more efficient (normally used for business applications).

systems software　Software used to run the operating system of a computer. Also known as **operating software**.

Tt

tab bar   Short name for tabulation bar. A device for moving to the tab sets that locate pre-determined positions on a typewriter or computer screen.

tab clear   A short name for tabulation clearing. A device on a typewriter or VDU screen for clearing all the pre-set tabulation stops.

tab set   Short name for tabulation set. A device on a typewriter or computer keyboard for setting new tabulation stops.

tabulating machine   A machine used in the punched card filing system which converts the holes on the cards into slots in places selected by the user. A tabulating machine is also a machine which can read data from one medium e.g. punched cards, to produce lists or totals.

tabulation   (1) The use of a machine to read data from one medium to produce lists or totals.   (2) The ability to move to a fixed place along a line rapidly and precisely. This facility, available on typewriters and VDU screens, is particularly useful for columnar work.

tabulation bar   A device for moving to the tab stops that have been pre-defined on a typewriter or VDU screen.

tabulation clear   A device on a typewriter or VDU screen for clearing all the pre-set tabulation stops.

tabulation set   A device on a typewriter or VDU screen for setting new tabulation stops.

Tannoy®   A commercial name for a type of public address system.

tape An input or output storage device for a computer. There are two kinds of tape: paper and magnetic. See also **paper tape, magnetic tape**.

Tape Callmaker One of the types of Callmakers offered by British Telecom for use over the telephone network. This Callmaker stores up to 400 names in alphabetical order, recording their telephone number on magnetic tape. Calls are made by moving the tape to the position containing the name required. The tape is power-driven to speed number selection. The hand set is lifted and the call button depressed. A separate dial unit is supplied to record or change stored numbers.

TD Callmaker One of the types of Callmakers offered by British Telecom for use over the telephone network. The TD Callmaker stores up to 31 numbers incorporating push buttons which can be used to input telephone numbers into a store or for making calls to numbers not stored. Also incorporated is a 'repeat last number' facility.

Telecom Gold Electronic mail system offered by British Telecom in the UK. Subscribers are given an electronic mailbox into which their messages are received and they can transmit messages to other subscribers.

telecommunications The transmission and reception of information electronically or electrically. Co-axial cables, broadcast radio and telephone lines are often used to facilitate transmission and reception between two or more terminals.

teleconferencing A conferencing system using telecommunications to enable meetings to be held with all participants linked. There are two main types: computer conferencing and video conferencing.

telecopier A device for the transmission of documents by telephone, where the sender has a machine which copies the document and transmits it, and the receiver has a compatible machine which reproduces the document sent. Also known as a **facsimile transceiver**.

telemessage An electronic mail service offered by British Telecom. Any message telephoned in to British Telecom by a pre-determined time will be delivered the next working day. A telemessage can be sent by dialling the operator and asking for the telemessage service.

telephone alphabet When words spoken over the telephone are in doubt and have to be spelled, the sounds of some letters are similar and can be distinguished by the use of a telephone alphabet e.g. when spelling out the postcode of PR3 1SA, the caller could say 'P for Peter, R for Robert, 3, 1, S for Sugar, A for Apple'. The Post Office has its own recommended alphabet, as does the Police Force for two-way radio communication.

teleprinter Resembling a typewriter, a device which is connected to a telephone line enabling messages at one end to be simultaneously reproduced on a machine at another end.

teletex A development of teleprinters, teletex is a system which transmits data between terminals at high speed over the telephone network, combining text editing with high speed telex-related equipment.

teletext Broadcast videotext. Information is carried from a computer to a receiver by radio waves where pages of information are displayed on a screen, the screen capable of being changed by a push button selection device. The two systems of this type in operation in the UK are Ceefax (British Broadcasting Corporation) and Oracle (Independent Broadcasting Authority).

telex A fully automatic teleprinter allowing interconnection between terminals over a dedicated network permitting communication in print. Each installation has an individual number and can identify itself by means of an answer back code. There is speculation that telex is likely to be superceded by teletex.

telex directory A directory of and for telex subscribers providing names, addresses, answer back codes, charges and services in the UK. Information about telex subscribers in other countries is available from their own official directory which may be purchased from the local area telephone office.

terminal A peripheral device consisting of a keyboard and screen, linked to a computer used to input data and receive output from the computer, or for sending and receiving data over a communications channel.

terminal digit filing A numerical filing system where the number allocated to a document or folder is a code for locating its exact position in a library. Digits are used in pairs and read from right to left e.g. a document numbered 654321 would be found on shelf number 21, in folder number 43 and would be document number 65 within that folder.

text A body of written or printed work.

text editing The editing of text on a computer, often within word processing. It may be carried out on any form of computer from a mainframe with appropriate software to a dedicated word processor.

text editor Software which manipulates the text of computer programs themselves. Modern word processing software is based on the original text editing programs although text editors are still used particularly for large computers.

text processing Computer editing and subsequent production of text. Often used as a synonym for word processing, although text processing more commonly refers to the handling of very large quantities of text.

thermal heat copier A process using heat instead of light to form a copy of an image with the use of a special heat sensitive copy paper. Although it is a very rapid method of copying, a disadvantage is that a thermal copier will not copy images unless they have a carbon or metallic content in them (which excludes most writing inks and ballpoint pens). Also known as **thermographic copier**.

thermal printer A method of printing using paper coated with a dye that darkens at predetermined temperatures to produce a copy of an image.

thermographic copier   A method of photocopying where heat is applied to the paper bearing the copy image to fuse the ink to the paper. As the ink is fused, it swells and the copy is produced with an embossed appearance. Also known as **thermal heat copier**.

three party connection   A telephone service available via the operator where three telephone lines can be connected simultaneously so that a three-way conversation can take place.

tickler file   A filing system used as a reminder system. Essentially a 'bring forward' filing system, where any topic which cannot be dealt with instantly is placed in a section of a numerically divided file. Numerical divisions are normally 1–31 for the days of the month. As the tickler file is checked daily, letters which were filed for attention seven days after receipt, will be picked up by the user to be dealt with.

tilt angle   A facility of some visual display units whereby the user can adjust the screen upwards, downwards, left and right to suit his or her angle of vision.

time sharing   A computer system that allows many terminals or users to concurrently share a central computer, each user having the impression that he or she has the sole use of the computer. Time sharing allows individuals or small companies to share the use of a computer which would be too expensive for them to purchase alone.

tone   (1) The shades of dark and light in an image relative to each other.   (2) A variety of sounds emitted from a telephone in use indicating dialling, engaged, number unobtainable or pay.

touch control   Refers to telephones with push buttons instead of a dial. Each number can be recognised by the different sound emitted as the buttons are pushed.

touch screen   A terminal with a screen which is sensitive to the touch of the user. Positions touched usually using a finger or a light pen are recorded by the computer as a signal allowing data to be input or a command to be followed.

track   A path along which data can be stored on a recording medium e.g. magnetic tape, magnetic disk.

transaction   In computing the processing of a record (e.g. the updating of a file) which incorporates the latest changes in a system.

transcribing machine   A machine which is capable of copying data from one storage medium to another with or without some form of translation.

transfer   The movement of data from one storage area or medium to another.

transfer box   In filing, a box used to transport and hold material being removed from an active file to a dead file.

transfer charge call   A call made over the telephone network for which the cost of the call is transferred to the recipient. A fee is payable for this service plus the usual cost of the call.

transparency   A sheet of acetate paper onto which diagrams may be drawn or documents photocopied for use in conjunction with an overhead projector. Transparencies are used as a method of presentation for groups, can be prepared in a variety of colours and retained in protective boxes for future use.

travel report   Information about motoring conditions (roadworks, traffic flow, road conditions) obtained by dialling a central number for an Automobile Association report.

treasury tag   Used as a method of holding documents together, a treasury tag is a small piece of cord with a metal clip attached to either end. The tag is passed through holes which are punched in the spine or left margin of a set of documents and the two ends of the tag tied together for additional security.

trunk call Another name for national calls. Most trunk calls can be dialled direct by means of STD to make a call to a number on another exchange. If the exchange required is not in the STD booklet, the operator should be contacted to connect the call.

trunk offering This facility allows the internal telephone operator or switchboard operator to signal an engaged extension that the operator wishes to speak or connect an urgent call. The operator must press a button which causes a rapid series of pips on the line. This interruption facility will normally be used for trunk or overseas incoming calls.

turnaround time (1) The time taken to reverse the direction of a transmission. (2) The time take between submitting a job to a computer and getting back the results.

twin drum duplicator A duplicator consisting of two drums which are connected by fabric. The fabric is inked by a roller with the ink being pumped from a tube attached to the machine. Twin drum duplicators are usually electrically operated. Compare with **single drum duplicator**.

typeface The design or style of characters produced by a particular printer or typewriter.

Uu

unconditional page break   A feature of word processing programs where the operator works through a document checking page breaks and putting in unconditional page breaks where necessary before printing the final version so that the final copy output is displayed effectively and correctly. Compare with **conditional page break**.

underscore   The term applied to the underlining facility on word processing software.

universal stationery   Stationery used by a company for any form of correspondence into which they may enter i.e. a letterhead is printed in bulk and can be used for business letters, orders, invoices, credit notes, estimates, statements, etc. It is more cost effective than using stationery which has been printed in order, invoice or credit note form, etc. although it does take the typist longer to produce the final document.

unobtainable tone   The term given to a telephone tone which, when the number has been dialled, is a continuous high pitched bleep. The unobtainable tone means that a telephone call cannot be connected because the number is either no longer in operation (unobtainable) or has been changed.

update   The process of amending the records in a file to show the current state of affairs e.g. when new records are added, old records deleted, or information within records is changed.

upgradeable   A term used to refer to hardware initially purchased which the user wants to update at a later stage e.g. a network system is upgradeable by the purchase of larger processing capacity which in turn will enable the installation of more terminals.

upper case   Capital letters of a fount, e.g. A as opposed to a.

user   The term given to the operator of a computer system.

user-friendly   Easy to use or self-explanatory software, particularly useful when unskilled or non-technical users need to access computer data. This usually implies the use of a high level programming language and sometimes graphical representation on screen.

utility   Software that can perform a particular task or routine without involving much work from the user, e.g. the copying of a document from one disk to another in which the user merely indicates which document is to be copied and the computer does everything else i.e. calculating the length of the document, examining the destination disk for storage, etc.

utility routine   The use of software which the operator can use for the manipulation of data e.g. file listing.

utility software   Programs provided by the computer manufacturer which perform basic functions such as file listing, card reading, etc.

Vv

validate   The checking of data to ensure that it is correct and that all pre-defined rules and regulations have been followed.

variable   Part of a computer program in which the data that has been stored or input can be subsequently changed. A variable has a name which does not change, and a value which can change.

variable block   A piece of information that can be substituted for another piece of information if requested by the user e.g. in the production of a standard letter, the operator will compile an address list and a form letter. The letter is fixed, but each line in the address list is a variable (i.e. subject to change). In the production of the standard when the computer encounters a variable, address lines will be automatically replaced from the address list.

VCR   Video cassette system developed by Phillips. The initials are used as an abbreviation of video cassette recorder.

VDU   Visual display unit. A cathode ray tube on which the output of a computer can be displayed.

verifier   A machine used for checking the punching of data onto punched cards in which the punched data is retyped.

verify   To check data which has been coded against data from the original source to detect discrepancies.

vertical filing   A method of filing where documents are filed in folders which are stood on the long folded edge, with the face side of the folder towards the observer in order of the classification adopted. The back edge of each folder protrudes beyond the front edge, allowing the user to either write or type the name of the file on the folder for easy identification.

video conferencing A form of teleconferencing where participants see as well as hear other participants at remote locations. Major cities can provide a suitable studio for public hire or private use.

video disk A disk containing recorded visual and sound information which can be played on a video recorder and transmitted to a television screen. In contrast to tapes in video cassettes, some video disks offer random access. At present, video disks can only play back pre-recorded information and are unable to record new information.

videophone A British Telecom facility where a small television screen is attached to the telephone and linked to the public telephone network enabling speakers to see each other.

video recorder A device which can be used to record and play back sound and pictures on magnetic tape when connected to a television set. The tape is enclosed in a cartridge. Also known as video tape recorder, video cassette recorder.

videotex An electronic system facilitating computer based information to be available via a VDU or appropriately adapted television set. There are two categories of videotex systems: (1) *Broadcast* videotex where information is carried from the computer to the receiver by radio waves enabling a limited number of pages to be displayed on a screen using a push button selection device e.g. Ceefax, Oracle. (2) *Interactive* videotex where information is carried from the computer to the receiver by cable, usually telephone lines. Instead of passively receiving information, users can individually interact with the computer e.g. Prestel. Also known as **viewdata**.

viewdata   Information transmitted to a user's television set through the use of telephone lines and television signals. Users can interact individually with the computer e.g. Prestel. Also known as **interactive videotex**.

visible book index   A filing system and a variation of visible card index where the edge of a book bearing an index is visible to the user. The index will display key details to aid the searching process.

visible card index   A filing system where cards are placed in trays overlapping each other. The edges of the card are visible to the user displaying key details to aid the searching process.

visible record computer   A small computer with a pre-stored program. Data is input manually and records are held in printed form on cards. Also known as **VRC**.

visual display unit   A cathode ray tube on which the output of a computer can be displayed. It can be used in conjunction with a keyboard or light pen as a means of accepting computer input. Sometimes referred to as video display unit and also known as **VDU**.

VRC   Visible record computer.

voice recognition   The ability of a computer to search in its memory for a match to words spoken in to it through a microphone by the operator. Also known as **speech recognition**.

voice synthesis   The ability of a computer to store sound patterns in its memory in order to produce simulated speech. Also known as **speech synthesis**.

voluntary deductions   One of two kinds of deductions made from a salary or wage. Voluntary deductions are made in consideration of contributions to sport and social facilities, sick pay schemes, savings schemes, etc.

Ww

wage Remuneration paid in return for employment. A wage is normally calculated on the basis of a working week or a stipulated number of hours.

wake up call A service offered by British Telecom whereby a subscriber can asked to be called at a specific time during the day. Also known as **alarm call**.

wallet A protective covering for the storage of single magnetic disks which is anti-static and which therefore protects the disk from contamination by dust.

weather report Information concerning the weather or weather-forecasting can be obtained over the telephone from the Meteorological Office. A user may find this a particularly good service when executives of a company have to travel to meetings or appointments in other areas.

White pages directory A British Telecom issue book which lists alphabetically telephone subscribers in the area where the book is issued by name, address and telephone number. Directories for areas outside the subscriber's area are available at an additional cost.

wide area network A generic term for the public telephone network and other networks in development allowing communications between distant points.

Winchester disk A form of backing storage for a computer consisting of a magnetic disk in an hermetically sealed container which is very powerful. The disk is sometimes referred to as a hard or rigid disk.

window A feature of some advanced microcomputer systems in which the VDU screen is split into sections, enabling the operation of different sections of the memory to be seen at the same time. Each section on screen is referred to as a window.

word count facility Found on some document-based word processing systems, the number of words typed at any one time appears on the screen. The facility is useful for people like authors who write to a specified number of words.

word processing The electronic storage, editing and manipulating of text using an electronic keyboard, computer and printer where text is stored on a magnetic medium except for final output which is in the form of print on paper.

word processor An electronic device used for the storage, editing and manipulation of text and consisting of a keyboard, an internal memory or storage, external storage, logic and printer. There are three main types: stand-alone, shared logic and distributed logic.

words per minute A measure of speed of transmission in telecommunications systems. Also known as **WPM**.

wordwrap A word processing term referring to the way in which a partially typed word is automatically moved to a new line if the length of the word proves too long to fit into the existing line. Also known as **wraparound**.

working disk In the event of a power failure or machine malfunction, a back-up copy of a disk is made and stored in a safe place. The original disk then becomes the working disk, i.e. the disk which is being worked on at the present time. If electrical, machine or operator error should then occur and the working disk damaged, the back-up disk can be used to make another working copy.

work station The combination of a keyboard, screen and processor to provide a facility for electronic office work e.g. electronic mail.

WPM   Words per minute.

wraparound   The automatic movement of a word onto a new line when the length of the word is too long to fit into the existing line. Often a feature of word processing software.

write   The process of recording information electronically. Writing to a disc means recording data onto a disk.

write protect   The covering of the exposed part of a floppy disk where information can normally be written to or read from, by a tag so that information can no longer be written onto the disk, but the reading of information from the disk is not interferred with.

write protect tag   A tag used to prevent data being written onto a magnetic disk.

WYSIWYG   Literally, what you see is what you get. The exact reproduction on a printer of graphics displayed on the screen of a visual display unit.

Xx

X-Press Callmaker One of the types of Callmaker facilities available from British Telecom. The X-Press Callmaker will store up to ten numbers of the operator's choice using push buttons instead of a dial. The push buttons have two separate functions; they can be used for making calls as on the normal push button telephone and, in conjunction with two additional buttons, they can be used as a Callmaker for calling any of the stored numbers. A 'repeat last number' facility is incorporated into this type of Callmaker.

xerography The technique of forming an electronic image onto a drum which is electrostatically charged to pick up a black powder. The powder is fused to the paper in the shape of the original image to form the final reproduction copy of the document.

XL Callmaker One of the types of Callmaker facilities offered by British Telecom. The XL Callmaker can store up to 46 numbers incorporating push buttons, which can be used either for making calls in the normal way or for putting telephone numbers into a store. Incorporating a 'repeat last number' facility, XL Callmakers have an inbuilt monitor loudspeaker which allows the progress of a call to be heard until it is answered.

Yy

Yellow Pages A British Telecom publication listing addresses and telephone numbers of local firms alphabetically classified by business or profession. The local directory is free to telephone subscribers and copies for other areas are available at additional cost.